Dancing with the Enemy:
Letting the Good Outweigh the Bad

By Meg Brown

Shirley,
Thank you for
all that you do.
Love to laugh
+
Live Each Day

This memoir is a work of non-fiction and is true in its entirety. Except for short explanations added for this book, journal entries were written on the dates shown.

For information, contact Motivated Proformance Inc., 628 Canyon Rim Dr., Dripping Springs, TX 78620.

www.megbrown.org
www.getumotivated.com

ISBN: 9-7809818525-1-5

First Edition, May 2006
Second Edition, February 2007
Third Edition, November 2008

Design: Joy Deborah Robison
Cover Design: Rick Clark

Publisher:

Comments from Readers

It was an awesome read. I felt propelled until the last word. It was a love story; a friendship story, an honest story, a family story, a sad story, an optimistic story, a real story, an exhausting story, a "how can one survive this" story. It becomes clear that Meg's love, honesty, and compassion are wrapped up in the rarest kind of beauty where inside matches outside.

Meg is extremely blunt with her thoughts and feelings in this journal and because of her sarcasm and brilliant humor, I cry like I've never cried before and with the next sentence she cleans it up and I'm laughing hysterically.

It was very moving, and sometimes heartbreaking, to read Meg's innermost thoughts about treatment and recovery. I think that cancer is one of those things you don't really understand unless you go through it. But I felt like I understood so much more when I read Meg's book. When she tells her story, it's moving and wonderful and totally hilarious.

Loved this book! Easy to read, interesting, uplifting—due to the happy ending.

I wanted to express how moved and inspired I have felt after reading Dancing with the Enemy: Letting the Good Outweigh the Bad, *and I want to thank Meg for further opening my heart and mind. She has touched many people's lives, including mine.*

It is honest, sad, tragic, motivating, and inspiring.

It was heartrending, funny, encouraging and reveals a young woman with tremendous endurance.

Dancing with the Enemy

Table of Contents

Acknowledgements

I want to thank all the people who helped me get this book in final form.

Thanks to Jane and Greg Friess for helpful suggestions, for editing and proofreading. Thanks to my readers, especially, Michael Landauer, Susie Treat, and Cindy Montgomery. Thanks to Erin Friess Pavlak for connecting me to Joy. Thanks to Joy Robison for her creativity in design. Thanks to Bryan Fiese and Susie Gold for all their advice and insight regarding motivational speaking and book publishing. Thanks to Bob Stevens for introducing me to Bryan and Susie. Thanks to Marc Pittman for visiting me that day and giving me words to live by.

Thanks to Dr. Brian Berryman, Dr. Charles Deur, and Dr. Michael Kasper for giving me this opportunity to be alive and well. Thanks to all my nurses at Seton Hospital in Austin, Arlington Memorial and Baylor University Medical Center in Dallas, as well as, Baylor's Blood & Marrow Clinic.

Thank you, Marco, for my life. Thank you, Lance Armstrong, for proving the body's resilience after cancer. Thank you, Oprah, for the hour each day which helped me forget I was sick and encouraged me to think about the future.

Thank you, friends, for always putting me first, always making the effort and always making my days better.

Thank you, Dad, for providing for your family and being our rock. Thank you, Matt, for making me laugh and for knowing when it was just time to love. Thank you, Mom, for being my editor, my secretary, my advisor, and, most important, my best friend. I love you all.

For I know the plans I have for you, says the Lord, plans for welfare and not for evil, to give you a future and a hope.

Jeremiah 29:11

I can see clearly now the rain is gone
I can see all obstacles in my way
Gone are the dark clouds that had me down
It's gonna be a bright bright bright bright sun shiny day
It's gonna be a bright bright bright bright sun shiny day

Oh yes I can make it now the pain is gone
All of the bad feelings have disappeared
Here is that rainbow I've been praying for
It's gonna be a bright bright bright bright sun shiny day

Written and originally performed by Johnny Nash in 1972.
Re-released in 1993 by Jimmy Cliff.
Lyrics are property and copyright of their owners.

Foreword

You have your story. Your friends have their stories. Everyone has a story. This book is my story. It begins when my life changed from one which was close to perfect—a childhood and adolescence full of love and success—to that moment when perfection disappeared forever.

In 2002, I entered my last semester in college like many other graduating seniors: thinking about what I was going to do with my life, questioning where I was going to live, wondering if I would find someone to be with forever. It was a busy time of life and it was a confusing time of life. Would I go straight into teaching? If so, where? Austin? New Zealand? Colorado? If not, would I just travel to exotic places and work odd jobs for a couple of years? It was time to visit the real world and to find out what I wanted to be when I grew up. As it turns out, I didn't need a passport or airline tickets or jobs to discover what I value above all else. And unlike many twenty-two-year-olds, it didn't take me long to figure it out. I had to learn fast because cancer was my teacher.

Just as my mother was recovering from breast cancer, I—a college athlete and seemingly healthy woman with endless opportunities ahead—met my future in the form of an eighteen centimeter tumor which had wrapped itself around my windpipe and heart.

Shortly after my mom's chemotherapy treatments began and about a week after the devastation of September 11, I picked up a journal given to me by Martha, a dear friend from grade school days. I hadn't written in it since 1995, but it was there when I needed a release from my worries. When rough times got even rougher, I needed it even more. Once I filled it up, I started another. In fact, nine journals record my life from September 19, 2001 until today.

So come with me through the days of my graduate course in what the real world can be. My journal takes you there in the moment. Live with me as I come to terms with my mother's illness and treatment, as I despair through months of misdiagnosis and worsening symptoms, as I face the accurate diagnosis of non-Hodgkins lymphoblastic lymphoma, the subsequent chemotherapy, the bone marrow transplant, and all the complications along the way. Read how I was buoyed in my dark times by people who loved me and those who helped me. Learn how I found the secrets to survive.

Meg Brown
May 2006

Chapter 1   September – October 2001

September 19, 2001:
Yesterday was the one week anniversary of the terrorist attacks. Baseball played again and things started to get back to "normal"—if that is possible. Mom started chemo yesterday. She will have 8 treatments every 3 weeks which will last about 6 months. They told her she will lose her hair in 7-14 days. Wow! That's a lot quicker than I expected. She is so strong…it will be tough, but she will do great. I am afraid to call today because I am scared she is sick.

September 22:
Friday, I ran errands all day. At Jiffy Lube, I talked to a group of men about the WTC attacks. They are scared like everyone else. Friday was Mom's 56th birthday. She said she was pretty tired. This was the first day she didn't feel "OK."

September 23:
I watched The Day of Prayer thing today. Oprah was in charge. I have spent the last few hours looking up Americorps stuff. I think that is what I want to do. It doesn't pay crap, but how rewarding. I'll have to discuss it with the parents, but I think I would really like it. OK, so I'm tired and my throat is killing me. Mom felt better today. She said she would feel "herself" in about a year. Damn.

October 8:
Saturday I got to see Mom. She shaved her head and it looked so cute. She is such a beautiful person. Today, her hair is starting to fall out.
On the news front, some man in Florida died from

anthrax and another is in the hospital. That phrase "Live Life to the Fullest" has never been truer. How blessed am I to have such a wonderful family and amazing friends. I love them so much.

October 29:
*I'm sitting at Zilker Park looking at a couple make out. Come on, get a room. Mom has been doing chemo for about 8 weeks. She goes in for her 3rd appointment on Wednesday. She has had some good days and some bad days. The past few times I have talked to her, she sounds pretty tired. Fatigue seems to be the main thing. She said she feels like such a wimp. She is not used to resting. I have no idea what she is going through. I just know it's extremely tough, but she will be better very soon. She is such a tough cookie. When people think of her, I know they are thinking of a strong, intelligent, cutie-pie, fun, sweet, and mentally healthy woman. She has it all. I'm so thankful she is my mom. To have one of your best friends be your mom is a special thing and Mom and I are extremely fortunate. She has 5 more treatments after Wednesday. One day at a time. I want to heal her. I want to take this disease from her. I have to admit—I keep thinking she is going to be just fine. I know she will be, but am I just taking her for granted? I keep forgetting that she has breast cancer. I forget that she is sick. I guess it's because I don't see her every day. When I think of her, I think energetic, go get 'em, and get out of my way. She will be fine. I just want her to be healthy **today**.*

Life since September 11th
Everything has changed. Life will be different forever. Anthrax is the new scare today. If it's some crazy American, that will be a slap in the face. We all pray for our soldiers.

We pray for our security. We are going to get through this. The question is when? And at what cost? That is the scary part. What else is going to happen? Smallpox? Bombings? Hijackings? How do we live? I know we don't know what is going to happen, but, damn, this sucks. I never thought things would be this way. Air marshals, soldiers in the airport, and such a widespread fear of flying because of someone's evil.

This is what I have been struggling with lately. Are we pre-destined? Could I die in a freak accident tomorrow? I have never thought about death more than I have since Mom's diagnosis and even more since September 11. Yes, I could die at 29 or 99. I know we don't know, but, damn, I just don't want to. I want to live every day with a purpose. In my life, I want to help people. Every day, I think more and more ANYTHING CAN HAPPEN. HAVE FUN. DON'T BE STUPID. HAVE FAITH. TAKE CARE OF YOURSELF, BUT CARE FOR OTHERS. Sometimes I think, Yeah…get in shape, eat good, look great…then, about 5 minutes later I think… Who cares? Eat whatever. Those 12 cookies could be your last. It's a confusing time right now. I have thoughts about life after graduation, my mom, our country, and what am I going to do as far as a career.

Traveling to New York

Lara and I have a ticket to NYC on December 27. Today, I feel good about it. That whole IF SOMETHING HAPPENS, IT WAS MEANT TO HAPPEN is a factor. I don't want to sit on my life, but I also have a lot of living left to do. If I don't feel comfortable, I won't go. But life was meant to be lived, right? I won't be stupid, but I want to live it.

5

Chapter 2

November 3
– November 20, 2001

November 3, 2001:

My friends Lara and Eryn and I ran in the Race for the Cure. It was so wonderful seeing the thousands of participants and thousands of survivors. Mom is doing well with her treatments. She is such a cutie without hair. During the race, I felt like my chest was going to explode. I have been having some trouble breathing when I run, but nothing like this. It was so tight. I don't know why. I guess I'm out of shape. Too many margaritas during the summer, I guess.

November 11:

Wow…my face is a bit swollen this morning. I guess I had too much wine at the wedding last night. That's some hangover—headache and a fat face.

Last week Blake (assistant athletic director at University of California, Irvine) called about a job. It sounds great. I have no idea what the hell I'm going to do after graduation. George Bush wants people to get involved in AmeriCorps. All of these decisions…

This week should be a good one. On Thursday, we are going to Waco for our Intramural Football Tournament. Then, I go home for a week. YES! I'm so excited to see Mom and hang out.

November 15:

My face has been puffy all week. I have no idea what the deal is. At first, I thought it was all of the wine I had at the wedding. But wine has not been in my diet the last couple of days. I went to the Health Center and they prescribed

Claritin, nasal spray, and inhaler. I have plenty of Claritin due to other visits, there is nothing in my nose that needs to be sprayed, and I'm not about to use an inhaler. Wasted trip…Oh, well.

Mom is doing so well. She's almost halfway done with her treatments. I'm so proud of her. She has stayed so positive and so strong. I don't know if I could do it.

November 17:

Puffy Face. Linebacker Neck. We think I might be allergic to feather pillows. Took Mom to her appointment. The doctor said she is doing great. She has her fourth treatment tomorrow. That means she is halfway done. I watched Oprah today. It was Thank You Day today. I cried like a baby. Most of the stories were about the victims of September 11. I have so many things to be thankful for. Please give my mom strength for her next treatment. Stay tuned for the Puffy Face outcome.

November 20:

Face is still fat. I have an appointment at 10:45 tomorrow. Who knows if they will be able to tell me anything? Mom had her 4th treatment today. She did great. So far—no sickness. They told her the next treatment will take 6 hours. DAMN.

Dad and I went to lunch today and we talked about life. What to do after college talk. I'm really leaning toward Americorps. I have written to them and I'm hoping to hear back from them in the next couple of days.

What am I thankful for? My family, Mom's strength and courage, Dad's heart and love for his family, Matt's determination and patience, Gram and Gramps—their sweetness, kindness, and love; my friends—they are all so *wonderful and care so much about me and my family; our country—we have united together to help one another get through this time of uncertainty; President Bush and staff— their decisions have been difficult, but worthy of our support; NYC's Fire Department and Police Department; the little things—sunny days, rain, music, sports, friendship, volunteers, good people, Oprah, shelter, food; faith—Lord, I'm so thankful for my Faith. Lord, thank you for allowing me and so many others to feel safe and secure with you by our side. I did not mean to put these very important people last, but I'm so thankful for our soldiers. God, please be with them and protect these brave people who are trying to protect us.*

Chapter 3   November 22, 2001
                                              – January 3, 2002

November 22:

Thanksgiving Day. The day with the family was great. The food was perfect. The day, however, was different. This was the first time I noticed the lack of buoyancy in Mom. She got tired at dinner and had to take a nap. Mom never needs a nap. The energy was just low which created a different atmosphere.

November 25:

I had the best time hanging out with the family. We all needed each other's energy. It was so much fun. Texas is going to the Big XII Championship game. Eryn's parents hooked us up with tickets. Love 'em. Good times ahead. I have a couple of projects due in the next few days, but I don't seem to give a rat's ass. Not the best teacher attitude. Oops…Oh, well.

December 3:

Just got back from Dallas this weekend. Chris Simms—not his best game. 3 interceptions and a fumble. We had a chance to go to the Rose Bowl and play for the National Championship. Damn. I feel bad for Chris. He is in a pretty rough spot. Mack Brown had him replace our god (Major Applewhite) and he did not need replacing. Other than the game outcome, it was a great weekend. Eryn and I went with Phil, a guy she is dating, and his friend Scott. We drank quite a bit and danced at my favorite place—HAVE A NICE DAY CAFÉ. The best '80s music. So much fun.

December 5:

Monday morning…Wake up…Hey, Puffy Face. Dear Lord, it was huge. I decided to go home to Arlington so I could get allergy shots on Tuesday and get back to Austin by that afternoon. Monday night, I tested out the inhaler. I either took too many puffs or took them too close together, but I definitely had a reaction. I woke about 2 a.m. and my neck is the size of an NFL linebacker's neck. I also have this shooting pain going from my shoulder down my arms. I described it as if my bones were metal and someone kept PINGING them. Damn, it was annoying and it hurt. I woke up Dad and he stayed with me through the whole thing. He is so awesome. Needless to say, no sleep Monday night. Got shots at 9 a.m. on Tuesday. Slept from 10 - 3 p.m. Took some steroids. Slept until 6. Stayed awake until 9 p.m. Slept from 9:30 -12:30 a.m. Couldn't go back to sleep. Left for Austin at 4:30 a.m. Two huge wrecks. The normal 3 hour trip took 6. Once I hit Austin, I went 5 miles in 3 hours. Almost peed on myself.

So, the face has gone down and I don't feel the need to sleep. I took a 2 hour nap today. But since 12:30 Wednesday morning, I've had 2 hours of sleep. It's now 2:40 a.m. Thursday morning.

Mom is doing awesome. Dad is solid. Love them.

December 7:

Graduation Day for several friends, mainly Eryn. My face is a mess. My eyes are puffy, face is fat, and my lips are huge. Hey, Angelina Jolie! I noticed some black stuff on my lips. That would be dried blood because my lips swelled so much during the night they cracked. Not a pretty day.

December 15:

I finished up my papers and projects for the semester. I came back to Arlington to get my health situation in order. Here's the update on that: I've got some allergy problems. Problems with mountain cedar and elm. Pretty much I'm allergic to everything. I got some more steroids and will take shots once a week. My face has not been as swollen the past couple of days. Dr. H. said the main concern is if my allergies get in the way of my breathing, then we have some problems. Good call, Doc. The breathing, though, has been good. The medicine is helping. Mom has 3 treatments left. She is doing so well. We think the reason for my asthmatic condition is psychological stress. In the span of 3 weeks, she was diagnosed, she had her surgery, and then came September 11. Mom and I talked about what a special thing she and I have going and it stressed me out thinking about losing that.

I am so pumped I have only one more semester of school. This summer my goal is to go to Colorado and work. In the fall, I am joining Americorps—hopefully I'll get accepted. I have heard so many positive things about it.

I'm quite awake right now. I had a 3 hour nap and steroids don't really calm me down much. Here goes the rambling: My goal for this last semester—Have so much fun. Enjoy college. Do the school thing but FOR SURE enjoy the friends. Lately, I've been thinking about crap that can happen to people. Why it happens to some people and not others. My mom, victims of 9/11, others with cancer, Sara Engelke (a high school teammate) and other car accident victims, or the coach who died in a random hiking accident. Why?

Then, I think of so many others—Gram and Gramps, Bill and Omega (married for 70 years), Chris (95-year-old golfer)…Yes, I am sure these people have had their rough spells, but I guess I just see them as alive which equals good things. I guess I just don't want shit to happen. I want to do so many things in my life. I want all of my friends and family to be safe and happy. Is that too much to ask?

This is another goal: Get in Shape. Get some Muscle.

December 23:

2 days before Christmas. 4 days before our trip. I am so excited. I got all of my allergy testing done. I'm allergic to cedar, dust (who isn't?), peanut butter, soy, baker's yeast, and the list goes on and on. I'm not allergic to apples or pot roast. THANK GOD!!! I think I am going to have to give myself shots. Pollen shots or something like that. That'll be fun. I guess no more PB sandwiches or peanut butter cups. Damn.

On Friday night, Mom and I talked about life. I had some questions for her about life and faith. We talked about her, September 11, living, and dying. I told her I was tired of thinking about all of the bad things that could happen. We talked about living life like you are going to live until you are 80, but living every day to the fullest. That's hard. I think I'm getting better with things. I am hoping my trip to NYC will settle my fears. New York is going to be awesome. We are going to Boston to see Erin for a few days, too. While in New York, I hope to see the Empire State Building, Ground Zero, a musical, Macy's, Central Park, and, oh, who cares. It's going to be so much fun.

Oh, yeah…some idiot on a plane from Paris to Miami had an explosive in his shoe. The flight attendant smelled sulfur, the asshole bit her, she called for help, and six guys and one huge basketball guy came to help her. They tied him with belts and sedated him. They don't think he was of Middle Eastern descent, but he was from Sri Lanka— wherever the hell that is. Moral to the story: people are still assholes. But others are brave enough to stand up to these people and aren't going to just sit there and let crap happen.

Mom & Meg, Christmas Day 2001

December 25:

What a great Christmas! It was so nice to be with family. I have to admit, it didn't feel all Christmasie the whole time. It was different this year. I think it's because we all appreciated what we have and that can't be wrapped. I didn't think I could be at home for two weeks and not go CRAZY. It's been absolutely wonderful. Mom was awesome. Mom today vs. Mom Thanksgiving = 2 totally different people. She was full of energy, smiling, and just having a great time. As far as my gifts go, they were perfect. Money, phone card, camera, and film. I am going to need it for my big NYC trip. Yahoo!

*We watched the concert for NYC tonight. How do these people do it? They were holding up pictures of loved ones, but they were still singing and smiling. Pisses me off that these people lost husbands, wives, dads, moms, sons, daughters, brothers, sisters, or best friends, and I get sad or worried about what **might** happen. That's a bunch of bull and a waste of friggin' time. I am not there yet, but I am getting better. Lara is coming over tomorrow because we leave in approximately T – 32 hours. Yeeeeeee-Haw.*

15

January 3:

What an unbelievable, fun time. Lara and I are sitting on the plane heading back to Dallas. This trip to New York was by far the most fun and the best vacation of my life. New York is a wonderful place. The people are great. I know it's different this year because of everything, but the people were so kind. We met so many people who were affected by September 11. One guy named T.J. knew 15 people who died, including two relatives. The firefighters we met lost 15 men and they found their captain's remains the day we met them. Jimmy, who worked downtown, ran through the ash that day. His sister's best friend lost her husband. Jimmy told me he thought he was going to die. It was so weird walking through the airport seeing men and women in uniform and carrying guns. I have to admit I was checking out everybody—like I could have done anything. Yes, I was being judgmental or profiling—whatever you want to call it. I did it. I think that is a natural response to what happened. After hearing the stories, all I could say and all anyone could say was May God Bless You and Take Care.

This was definitely the best trip to date. Lara and I had an absolute blast. I love that girl. To many more trips to come.

Lara, Meg, Erin in Connecticut December 2001

Chapter 4   January 22 – February 18, 2002

January 11:

My face is still puffy in the morning. I don't understand. Sometimes I'm like, "Is this really allergies?" It has to be because I don't feel bad. I'm giving myself 3 shots a day and taking prednisone. These shots will work. I know they will. I'm not eating some of the foods—scratch that—any of the foods I truly love. No chips, cookies, brownies, wheat thins, peanut butter—yeah, I've lost a little bit of weight. I weighed 144 this morning. I haven't weighed that since I was about 15. I've been getting some skinny ass comments. It's kinda funny.

January 20:

What's going on with me? I've got a puffy face, puffy eyes, and puffy lips. Would you please go away! The cedar count is like 20 times the norm. I'm just getting annoyed with it.

Got graduation stuff in the mail the other day. So excited.

Life after May—Working a camp near Philadelphia for the entire summer. Runs until mid-August. After that, hell, no idea. Americorps seems to be fading out. I think I want to make some money. I talked to this guy about Americorps and he said some love it. Other don't. Depends on what you take from it. Here is one of the kickers. It's for people between 18 and 24. I think the majority would be 18-year-olds trying to pay for college. Really don't want to be with a group of 18-year-olds who are not sure how to work for ten months. That sounds snooty, but that is what I am feeling.

Other options: Teaching Abroad. New Zealand. Dawn's

friend has a place to stay. But Dawn (a student in my teaching cohort) is only going for about 3 months. If I go, I am going to teach for a whole year. I keep thinking…why not? I'm young. How fun would that be! I would learn about different ways to educate. New Zealand might have some ideas we could adopt in America. Since I don't have a job there yet, it's hard to commit. My other options would be to move to New York, Colorado, or California and teach. Getting up and moving to one of those places is a little easier to swallow than New Zealand. We'll see. First, I have to see if I can afford it. Second, I have to get a job. This planning for life after college is tough. I know one thing for sure. No more school. The thought of going back to school kinda makes me sick to my stomach.

January 25:

Today's topic is life after August 19, 2002. That's the day I finish up at camp in Pennsylvania. Dad and I had one of the many, "What the hell are you going to do?" talks this evening. Those are always fun. I tried to make something up this time, but that didn't work out too well. We both said things, but as far as getting anywhere, I don't think we did. "What do you want to do?" the man keeps asking. I stare blankly. Does he want me to answer? Does he want me to sit there and look like I'm really pondering the question? Or should we both watch the TV on mute? I'll take door #3.

*For real, let's get this part out of the way. What do **not** want to do? I don't want to go to school anymore. I'm tired of it. I do not want to be a flight attendant, doctor, lawyer, nurse, professor, school counselor, or college coach. The corporate world does not appeal to me much, either. This is good since I have eliminated the school option. What do I want to do? I'll start with what I like. I love people. I love* kids. *I love making people smile and feel good. I love to travel. I love sports, the outdoors, and I love to see people smile when they have learned something. Oh, I can just feel all of the career opportunities. Looks like teaching, coaching, teaching, or coaching.*

Here's what I **DO** *know for sure: I graduate on May 18th at 10 a.m. in Gregory Gym. I need to be in Pennsylvania for camp on May 28th and I'm there until August 19. Should be a great time. A job around September 1st would be splendid.*

My health seems pretty good. It's getting better. I'm still taking the steroids. My face does not get as puffy, but I still have the raspy voice. Other than all of that crap, it's a lot better.

Mitra and Puffy Face Meg at Carnival in Austin

February 2:

Time to vent. This is fucking bullshit. I looked like a damn alien this morning. My eyes are puffed out, my face is swollen, my lips are protruding, my throat is fat, it's hard to fucking breathe, and there is some shit going on with my tongue. Damn. When will all of this shit be over? For real, what the hell is wrong with me? This is not normal. I'm still taking steroids. Are they helping? The only time my face is not puffy is when I sleep on 2 or 3 pillows. What the hell is that all about? Why haven't I gotten better? Cedar fever, cedar fever, blah, blah, blah…bullshit. My hormones are all jacked up. Had my period 3 times in a month. That's dandy. I'm afraid I'm going to start growing chest hair pretty soon. Do I really have asthma? How the hell did that happen? The girl who could run forever has fucking asthma? When I do try to run, I can go for about 3 minutes before I start wheezing. That's BULLSHIT.

I was excited about getting sleep today, but too bad the pressure in my face keeps me from sleeping. Shit. Oh, and it's hard to breathe. So, what to do? Go workout and pray that no one is in the workout room? I don't like scaring people. Or do I sit on my ass and wait for all of the shit in my face to drain back into my lungs? Tough Call.

OK. I feel better. I know I shouldn't complain about this. Mom has to get chemotherapy every 3 weeks. She gets shots every week for breast cancer. People I know have things worse than damn puffy eyes to worry about. It's just so damn annoying. SHIT. Okie, Dokie…done with that.

Tonight Mitra and I are going to Carnival—Brazilian Mardi Gras. I have heard it is a blast. Good thing is—I can wear a mask.

Mom is doing good. She has one more treatment. She has done so well. She's just amazing. OK, I'm about to go and pop 2 steroids so I can swallow. DAMMIT.

Oh, for the record, I exercised. Feel better. Said the f-word to Mom about 10 times. Not your best. Face is still puffy—could do without that. Oh well.

February 7:

Who has a yeast infection in her mouth? That's me. What in the hell? Stupid ass prednisone. I am not a fan of that stuff. My face is breaking out, it's pretty puffy, and I have my period about every 7 days. Good times—not so much.

I'm just going to hang out this weekend. I haven't felt like going out lately. Why did I start cleaning the apartment at 1 a.m.? Damn Steroids.

February 10:

Today, my face hurt because it was so fat. I am going to have to stay on the meds to control the symptoms even though I'm afraid the steroids are giving me the puffy face. I don't know what the hell to do.

February 13:

What a glorious day! Mom's last treatment was today. I'm so happy for her. I don't think I really know what she went through. She is a tough lady. When I would talk to her, I would have to remind myself that she was taking chemo.

The face, dear Lord, was fat this morning. I'm talking embarrassingly fat face. "Who is that?"-FAT. Oh, well, it's going to get better soon—I pray.

February 18:

On Valentine's Day…uhhhh…no date. I went to Trudy's with my wonderful girlfriends. Got a little intoxicated. Oops. That night I didn't sleep and couldn't breathe too well. I'm getting up every hour and coughing up blood. I get up for good at 4 a.m. and wait for time to pass. My throat is swollen and SURPRISE! I look like crap. I go to the health center. My face is fat and red, the skin is blotchy, the eyes are gross, and I feel like crap. I don't think this is from the Mexican Martinis.

My dad decided to come down and play nurse. The next day I see Dr. C. This new allergist told me to stop everything I have been doing with the other allergist. He was shocked at the idea of me giving myself shots and being on prednisone for 2½ months. He thinks I have had a reaction of some kind, whether or not it's allergic?—we don't know. He said I don't have congestion in my chest, but in my throat. Agree. When I breathe, my throat literally gurgles. I have always said, "There is so much crap in my throat." When I wake up, it's like I have a pool ball in my throat. They are discussing throat x-rays and me going to an ear, nose and throat doctor. Dad and I leave his office feeling good about my three new inhalers and other medicine.

Here's what sucks. We trusted Dr. H (the hometown allergist) which is what we were supposed to do. You trust your doctors. But for 4 months, nothing has changed. I'm not even sure if I have allergies. If we treated me for allergies for 4 months and have gone nowhere, do I have allergies? The question of the frikin' year.

I have missed two days of school and I'll have to make that up at the end of the year. That's OK. I need to get better. The last straw was when I warmed up with 1st graders and I couldn't breathe.

I took the Excet test to get my teacher certification on Saturday the 16th after about 4 hours of sleep. Before the test, I had a scary moment. I took a bite of an egg taco and my throat closed up. I couldn't breathe. It felt like minutes. I really didn't want to die going to take this dang teacher test. The test—sure going to have to take that one again. I fell asleep after every question. I had no idea what I was doing. I looked like I was on crack. I was going to say hi to this girl in the bathroom, but I saw myself in the mirror. She would not have recognized me.

As I bring this journal to a close, let me note what significant things are going to happen.

—Mom will get the green light on February 27.

—I'll start student teaching

—Go to Cali for Spring Break

—Getting well

—Graduate

—Find a Job

It's going to be a busy time, but it'll be fun.

March 7:

State your location: Sitting in my bed, watching TV, looking at the beautiful Austin view. Too bad I'm in room 703 at Seton Hospital and I have CANCER. SHIT.

So, let's recap the 16 days since my last entry:

February 19:

Dad goes home after the doctor's appointment. I have improved and have x-rays tomorrow and I will see the throat doctor on Friday.

February 20:

Go to school and face is fat. Coughing all day and breathing is difficult. It feels like someone is pumping air into my neck and face. My face keeps getting bigger and redder and I'm feeling like total shit. I call the doctor and tell them I need x-rays TODAY. I will wait for the x-rays and take them to the doctor that day. As I'm filling out my info sheet, I start crying. It isn't that ugly cry face, just tears. I think I knew this was really bad. Get my x-rays and tell the technician that I think I should check into the hospital because I don't think I'll be able to breathe tonight. The radiologist calls me into his office. He asks me when was my last chest x-ray. I told him this is my first one. He says I have a lot of junk in my lungs. He says my trachea looks to be about ¼ of the normal size and we should be able to see my heart and we can't. He says all that white stuff could be from the prednisone, or mucus build up, or a TUMOR. Do not want to hear that one. Tears. Ugly cry face. He tells me the ER is expecting me and I need to go there right now. Call

Eryn. Call Dad. Go to the ER. Tracy and Aunt Barbara meet us at the ER and we wait, wait, and wait some more. My shoulders are falling asleep. I cannot feel my feet. The nurses try to draw blood but can't get any blood return. My face is a shade of purple. Looking back, I was extremely close to the edge. Finally, we see some doctors. One tells us this MASS could be lymphisomething which is good or Hodgkins. I really do not know what all of this means. I ask Mom and she says the word cancer. Another word I do not want to hear. SHIT. He tells me they will do a biopsy tomorrow to figure out what all is happening. Another doctor comes in and tells me I have a lot of fluid around my heart. He points to my drinking cup which is about a 6 oz cup and the fluid around the heart should barely cover the bottom. I have 2 cups. Damn. At this time, my face is almost purple. My neck is fat and hard. The pulmonary doctor says I sound like Darth Vader. He really could not get over the fact that my face is so fat. We finally get to a room around 11:30 p.m. I go to sleep, sitting elevated, oxygen tubes in my nose, with my fat face, and wondering if I have cancer.

February 21:

Got some testing done that morning, breathing treatments, pep talks, and went into surgery for the biopsy around 2. The docs told my parents and me about a possible complication. Because my trachea is so small, the anesthesia might deaden things and stop my breathing altogether. When I went to sleep, my muscles around the trachea would relax and the airway could shut down and close up. That is why my body would not let me go to sleep and why I would cough all night. It was my defense mechanism. Scary shit. If this complication occurred during surgery, they would have to be prepared enough to put a hard tube down the trachea or use something to revive me. This actually happened twice: once at the beginning going under the anesthetic and once coming up at the end. The danger in this is brain damage or something. Thank the Lord they were ready.

Diagnosis: I have an 18 cm tumor in my mediastinum. It's pressing against my trachea which is why I can't breathe. It's wrapped around the vein that drains blood from the face—hence puffy face. Non-Hodgkins lymphoblastic lymphoma—apparently not the good kind. Whatever that means. They said because it is a fast and aggressive cancer and they must treat it as acute leukemia. I started chemo that night.

I got to recovery and things are real fuzzy. I did not hurt any where—I don't think. I had a drain running from my heart to get rid of the fluid. I had IVs everywhere and because the tumor was so close to my heart, they couldn't put the groshong catheter up there. So, they put one in the groin of my right leg. They use this catheter for the infusions and injections so I don't have to have needles stuck into me every other minute.

Hello. My name is Meg Brown. I'm 22 and I have Cancer. I feel like I am at an AA meeting.

I am now in ICU, peeing in bed pans—not so fun—and what I remember the most about that first day was I could not drink any water. Holy Cow, I wanted water. My lips were on fire. I could only get ice chips. Come on…throw me a bone here. My nurse was cute. His name was Brian, so that was a plus.

I really did not feel much pain when I was in ICU. Fatigue was the main thing. But the perfect medicine was all of the visitors. They said there were about 30 people in ICU. It has been amazing. I'll talk more about that later. I stayed in ICU until the 23rd and got my room. 703.

That first night in ICU right after the oncologist told me I had lymphoma, I dictated a letter to Mom to read at Fast Break on Senior Night. It was a good letter and I heard she did great. I heard there was not a dry eye in the place. I wanted the Longhorn basketball fans to know what was going on and I wanted them to know that I need their prayers and positive thinking. I told them chocolate is definitely an acceptable gift. Oops. Should have asked for money. I've got chocolate growing out of my ass.

February 22:
Dr. Kasper, the oncologist, did a bone marrow biopsy. They could not put me under because of the breathing complications. That felt weird. They deadened a spot on my butt and I could feel him grinding. It did not really hurt—it was just weird. He had trouble because my bones were so strong.☺ The cancer is in the blood or the marrow or something like that. I don't really understand the lingo just yet. The days are running together. I haven't gotten that sick. I just don't have an appetite—especially for this nasty hospital food. I think one morning I threw up, but it was not that bad.

February 23:
I'm in my room and have already received so many presents, journals, books, chocolate, magazines, candy, stuffed animals, hugs, kisses, encouraging words, prayers, and people. It has been fun seeing all of my friends and good people.
The doctors told me I will receive 11 chemo treatments in 14 days. Damn.

February 26:
The doctors told us good news. This cancer is curable and I'm

responding to the chemotherapy. I had a spinal tap that day. That was different. Dr. Kasper took fluid out of my back and then put chemo back in. This is to make sure no lymphoma cells get into my spinal fluid. I'm all clear in that department so far. Side effects are headaches and, damn, does my head hurt, especially when I cough. Vicodin, Tylenol, nothing helps.

February 27:
Not the best day. Breakfast was a cinnamon roll, oatmeal with peaches, and canned pears. No thanks. What healthy person would want that? Lunch was a turkey sandwich. One bite, yak…yak…yak. Not so fun.

Got my groshong changed. They put this one above my right boob. Again, no anesthesia or maybe they just gave me a little. As I was going to the OR, they asked me if I was loopy or tired. No, not at all. I don't think I was numb at all during the procedure. I felt every poke, every grind, everything. Felt a little weird and it kinda hurt.

Sat on my butt, fell asleep when company was here, and then I take a shower. Mom and I are washing and I say, "Mom, I am starting to get light-headed." Things get bright and I start seeing spider-web designs. I dream about something (don't remember), but I faintly remember Mom screaming, "I NEED HELP IN HERE!" I hear nurses screaming my name and feel my legs and arms shaking. The first thing I see is Mom leaning up against the wall crying. I tell them I am OK. Apparently, my mom saw my eyes roll back, the color go out of my face, I hit my head and then I started shaking. It looked like I was having a seizure. I scared Mom to death. I now have to get an MRI to check and see if my brain is OK. This MRI thing is in the tunnel. They keep asking me if I am claustrophobic. I am so tired that I fall asleep. There are these loud noises. Jack-Hammer noises. I am quite relaxed because I am so tired. Not my best day.

March 1:

A great day. I felt so good. I had a constant flow of visitors. Kenva, my hairdresser, came around 8 p.m. to chop my hair. When she got here, I was so tired. She cut the ponytail and trimmed for about 2 minutes. I told her I was getting tired and needed to take a break. So, she did not finish and I now have a mullet. Not so cute.

Meg's Mullet Haircut

March 3:

I've been feeling good. So many visitors. They were almost forming a line in the waiting area out by the elevators. Mom or Dad or Matt would usher 2 or 3 in at a time. They were UT athletes, coaches, professors, girls who lived in the dorm when I did, acquaintances I had met through friends, high school friends, former coaches. It was the most amazing thing I've ever seen. Got tired and fell asleep about 8 both nights. On one of those days I had a blood transfusion and a fever. The transfusion made me feel better, but they really did not want me to get a fever.

March 4:

We have decided to cut the number of visitors which has helped with the fatigue tremendously. It was a pretty good day. They told me the tumor is shrinking. This day was the day I had 10 wonderful minutes. The doc came in and said my x-rays looked clear. I asked what clear meant. He said no pneumonia and my mediastinum is almost normal. So the tumor is almost gone—Yee-Haw. Then a preacher came by and read some scripture and said a wonderful prayer. Then 2 minutes later WNBA star Cynthia Cooper called. She was at the Big XII basketball tournament and someone told her about me. She said she is praying for me and thinking about me. She said to tell my mom she said hello—her mom died of breast cancer. She told me to stay positive and know I can beat this thing. It was awesome. It lifted me up for the rest of the day. Awesome day.

March 8:
I just got done talking with Cole Pittman's dad, Marc. Cole was a UT football player who died in a car accident in February 2001. We talked about making something good out of this bad situation. We talked about how there are going to be good days and bad days, but hold on to the good days. He told me to make a difference. He said that after this experience I will be more sensitive to others and will know when they are hurting. He stressed that the struggles in life are through the mind. Agree. It was a wonderful conversation with a wonderful man.

I'm now going to break this experience into a few segments.

Treatments: *Dr. Kasper, the oncologist here, said he would treat me like this: 6 - 8 months of chemo and then a bone marrow transplant and that would take a year. Barf. I did not really expect to hear that "year" part. I asked him about the chemo. I was thinking the treatments would not be as heavy as this initial blast. WRONG. He said they will be*

31

just as powerful and I will probably have to go into the hospital several times. Oh, well. We'll jump that bridge when we get there.

*   **People:** *The nurses and doctors have been wonderful. One ICU nurse gave me a sign language book because I mentioned I wanted to learn sign language. That was so nice of her. They have just been great and the x-ray boy downstairs—Drew—is such a cutie.*

*   *Oh yeah…I finished the new haircut. It's cute. It won't be there for long.*

*   **Family:** *Absolutely wonderful. Matt—so funny. Geeze, he is funny. He has been such a relief and so positive. He calms Dad and makes everyone laugh. Dad—struggling. He wants to control things and control his family. The last thing he wants is for his family to get hurt. He lost his mom to cancer. It blew him away when Mom got cancer. He can't believe that I have cancer and he is pissed. He has cried a lot and was pretty low for a few days. He wants me to help him with his faith. I will, but he has to let me. It's not just faith in God. He has to have faith in people. For example, a few days ago, he was driving me crazy. He did not want anyone to come visit. He took the phone off the hook and was just being a pain. Just because he would rather be isolated from the group does not mean that's what I want. People and friends are my medicine. He is doing better. He cleaned out the apartment and took everything back to Arlington. I love him so much and I hope our relationship can grow through this thing. Mom—amazing. She is all clear. I can't believe we found out our diagnoses 6 months apart to the day. CRAZY. She was hurting at first because 1) her little girl has cancer 2) she did not feel like she listened to me back in November when I said I wanted a chest x-ray. She is so strong and we are going to have a good time through this. I don't think she*

will, but she does not need to wear herself out taking care of me. I love that lady.

Friends: *Wonderful. I have a fabulous inner circle of friends. They are wonderful people and I love them so much.*

Me: *I am feeling great. How am I sick? I know chemo helps, but it is the thousands and thousands of prayers. I feel like I'm sitting on a carpet and just floating along because so many people are lifting me up. I am not scared. I am not mad. I am not sad. I am comfortable. I am peaceful. I am determined. I am happy. I have been having fun these past few days seeing all of my friends. I know this is going to be long, but I know I can do it. I have to. I would rather be fighting this than not. I know heaven is great, but I'm not ready to check it out just yet. I plan on getting some things accomplished during this thing. Sign Language, reading some books, speaking events, writing a book, and getting on Oprah.☺*

What is next? We are waiting for my counts to go up. My WBC (white blood cell) count was 0.1 the other day when normal is 5 - 10. Oops. Today, it is 1.7. The docs are feeling I'll be ready to leave by Wednesday. It's Friday. Oh my gosh, I would really like to go home—or at least see the sun. I will start off seeing Dr. Deur, my mom's oncologist, but we are going to get a few other opinions. I guess that's called learning from your mistakes. That is the plan so far.

March 9:

Saturday morning. Day number 5 of feeling great. My counts are rising. It looks like Tuesday or Wednesday will be the day to go home. Yesterday I took some candy down to ICU (in the wheelchair). Katie and I took some walks. The days have been smooth. But I WANT TO GO HOME. Today I'll write some thank you notes and hang out. My hair is falling out. I'm giving that another week. Good times.

Because my friends are one of the reasons why I am alive today, they deserve more than just a passing mention. I've already introduced my roommate Eryn and three wonderful friends—Lara, Tracy and Katie. Now I am going to tell you a little bit about them.

ERYN was my roommate for four and a half years. She was a good roommate and teammate. Neither of us were neat freaks. We weren't into decorating or cleaning with antibacterial stuff unless necessary. Necessary usually meant mold. Eryn is a positive person who works hard and has a good sense of humor. She was always fun and teamed up with me on various practical jokes. Our disagreements were rare in our four-plus years together.

Eryn knew something was wrong with me way before I went to the hospital in February 2002. I remember her telling me that she heard me breathing while I was taking a nap, and I sounded like an 80-year-old man with emphysema. She almost called the hospital right then. It was her graduation I attended when I had the Angelina lips. Her first reaction was, "Whoa," followed by "maybe we won't see anyone."

She was the first one I called when I needed a ride to the ER. She didn't ask any questions. I knew she was scared because I looked horrible. After telling her it was a tumor, I remember her saying that day, that night, and that week, WE'LL BEAT IT. Eryn would do anything for me.

LARA worked in the women's basketball office my senior year. Lara was one of the team's biggest fans. After basketball season, I looked forward to the opportunities to hang out with non-athletes. Lara was my first choice. Because she was always happy, she loved laughing, and she never met a stranger, I wanted to be around her. Like me, Lara had plenty of friends. I met dozens of people through Lara who all prayed for me and supported me. Lara, her friends, my friends and I went out just about every weekend. Lara introduced me to her kind of college life and I loved it.

When I got sick I had not known Lara a year, but it was like we were sisters. One word to describe Lara through this is loyal. With loyalty, came love, hope, humor, and more love—so maybe not just one word. Lara would do anything for me.

TRACY was a teammate for three years at The University. Because she was a year younger than me, she was playing her senior year while I was finishing up my degree and fighting the "allergies." Tracy became one of my closest friends on the team. Because of our friendship, Tracy's Aunt Barbara and Uncle Joel became my aunt and uncle, too. Their door has always been open to me.

In my playing days when I became frustrated about basketball, Tracy was the friend I turned to. When I was frustrated with the Puffy Face look, I turned to Tracy. Tracy is honest. Tracy is mentally healthy. Tracy is loyal. During my years of illness and recovery, she always checked in on me, and she always prayed for me. Tracy would do anything for me.

KATIE was a teammate in college—a funny one. Katie and I share a love for sports, and we would always talk about our philosophies on whatever game was playing. Katie comes close to being the only girl who knows more about football than I do. She can throw a football better than most guys, too. Katie makes me laugh. Katie and I can talk about anything. Katie's then fiancé **FRANK** sold surgical instruments in the hospital where I was staying. He came by every day just to say, "Hi." Katie and Frank helped Dad load up all my boxes and furniture from my apartment to the rental truck for the move to Arlington. They didn't have to do this; they didn't get paid. They did it because they love me. Katie and Frank would do anything for me.

Eryn, Brenda, Tracy with Meg at Seton Hospital

With permission from Coach Conradt, Mom read my letter to the fans at Fast Break after the final game of the 2002 Lady Longhorn season on February 23rd, a victory against Texas A&M:

Hello to all. This is Meg Brown. I played basketball here for four years. The last thing I want to do on this special night is steal the stage from the seniors—Asha, Dana, Kenya and Tracy.

Although politics has never been my thing, for the next few minutes I'm gonna do some politickin.' Here we go.

I'm going to give you a quick reflection of my life the past four months and then I'll focus on today. At the end of October, I had trouble breathing when I was running. A few weeks later, I woke up after a wedding and my face was bloated. Since the bloat lasted for weeks, I figured it wasn't the wine. We began to suspect I had developed Austin allergies.

Not so much.

After three months of testing, shots, whiffers and hocus pocus, we decided to get another opinion. Within a week, the new doctors discovered I have lymphoma—a type of cancer in the lymph nodes. So it isn't allergies. It is a mass of goo that has successfully wrapped itself around my trachea and the veins and arteries near my heart.

Almost done with the gross details.

Thursday (2/21/02), doctors at Seton performed a biopsy and drained the fluids. This is what we found. I've a helluva fight on my hands.

But by the time you hear this I will have already started chemotherapy. So the fight is on.

Here's where you come in.

For four years, I felt nothing but genuine love from all the people in this room. I know when I ask you to help, you will. I need your help. I ask that you pray and think positive thoughts. Starting today until the day I'm back playing pickup games. I ask that you see light shining on me and that you have me wrapped up in your healthy hands.

By no means will this be an easy battle. But I will win. And it will be a helluva lot easier with y'all on my team.

I like how my mom described all the people in my life in this unfortunate situation. She said being part of this much love is awesome even when events are gruesome. Maybe heaven is awesome love without the hell.

To those of you without Kleenex or old shirts and who have already used the tablecloths, I apologize.

There is good news. Since I'm not allergic to food, chocolate is acceptable.

To all the girls and the staff, I love y'all. Best of luck the rest of the year.

In conclusion, excuse my language, but I'm gonna kick this thing's ass. I expect nothing short of that attitude from you all, my teammates, and my family.

To everyone, thank you. God Bless and Hook 'em, Horns.

With love,
Meg Brown

JODY CONRADT was my coach in college. She was inducted into the National Basketball Hall of Fame in 1998. She did not earn that honor by being a pushover. I remember thinking after being diagnosed, "If I can survive Coach Conradt for four years, I can beat cancer." Coach did her job by pushing us to be our best every day.

When I was in the hospital, coach visited four or five times. She always knew how long to stay, what to say, and what to do. She gave me a huge, framed team poster. I hung it in the hospital room. She checked in on me a couple of times a month after I left Austin, and always asked if I needed anything. She gave my mom permission to read my letter to the Texas fans after the last home game. Coach would do anything for me.

March 10:

I'm going home. Yesterday was a good day. I saw a lot of people. Kinda drained me. We also found out possible treatments. If I were to stay here, I would start Round #2 and be in the hospital for about 4 days. Not fun. That coupled with my hair falling out kinda brought me down a little bit. This morning we are just packing up and waiting for the doctor to come in and say Peace Out. I'm very ready to go home, but I'm going to miss my friends. But we gotta do what we gotta do.

This morning I had a little cry with Mom. I think I saw the length of this tunnel and that pissed me off. I know there are going to be some ups and downs, but like Mr. Pittman said, "Let the good outweigh the bad." Round #2 starts Friday. Sheesh.

March 11:

Oh, the first day at home. Not too bad. Went to bed last night at 8 p.m., peed about 5 times in the night, woke up at 8, and then took a nap around 10. I'm so lazy. J Slept for a couple of hours, talked on the phone with a few buddies, and just woke up from another nap. I feel pretty good, just tired. My body hurts. It feels like I have been in a car wreck or someone has jumped on my body with spike heels for two days. My fingers don't have much feeling in them either. I didn't think all of this stuff would happen at once. Anywho…here is the deal: Going back to the hospital Friday. Damn. Can we get a break? Guess not. Here's what I'm hoping—go to the hospital for a couple of days and then recover at home. That would suck if I was in the hospital for two weeks and out for a week. But I am not in control—not so much. Shaved the head today. Got a few too many moles. About 8 too many. One is really huge. Mom and I with our bald heads are quite the pair. YIKES!

Mom & Meg

March 12:

Yesterday marked 6 months past the World Trade Center attacks. That is still so unbelievable. Whenever I start to think about my situation, I remember that I am here and I have a chance. Those people on September 11th weren't given a chance.

Today has been pretty good so far. Woke up around 8 and tried on Mom's wig. HILARIOUS. There is no way someone would look at me and think that was real hair. We got the biggest laugh out of that. I feel good, just tired. The body is not as sore. I still have this cough and when I breathe, my throat makes this raspy noise. It's not like it was, but it's still there. I guess I expected the tumor to be gone and breathing to be normal. I know the tumor won't grow back, but I'd really like it dead…for sure.

Dad and Brenda are working in my room and putting the bed together. I know I can't do much, but I still feel helpless. My crap is everywhere and I'm a little worried Mom might wear herself out. Speaking of worried—Dad is worried I am going to get bored…which is very possible, but at least give me a chance to get bored. He's so cute. He came in this morning and asked if I've been doing my prayers. Yeah! I'd be an idiot not to. Or if I've started reading some books. Uhhhh, not yet. Give me a couple days to get used to this and then I'll take on a few projects.

March 14:

Yesterday I went to see Dr. Deur. Waited for about 3 hours. Here's what he said in a nutshell:
- *Impressive Mass*
- *6 months of treatment*
- *8 rounds of chemo…3 weeks apart…probably go to the hospital every time*
- *Rounds 1, 3, 5, 7 will be 4 bags of cytoxan, a 24-hour drip of Adriamycin, handful of steroids (the kind that break down muscles not build them up), and a shot of vincristine—directly into the spinal column.*
- *Rounds 2, 4, 6, 8 will be methotrexate and ara-c, plus leucovorin, which will help my body recover from all the 'poison' it will be getting.*
- *16 frikin' lumbar punctures (spinal taps)*
- *talk about bone marrow transplant and radiation later*
- *treatment is tough.*

I left the office and I think it hit me that this is for real. I don't think I realized how tough the treatments were going to be. It just kinda sucked thinking about having good days when it might really just be good hours. I was pretty bummed after the visit. Took a nap, of course, and then Jill P. and

Jennifer O. (high school buddies) came over. I had such a great time laughing with them. They pepped me right up. People are my medicine.

March 16:

I'm waiting on my spinal tap. It's 9:25 a.m. on a Saturday morning. I'm hooked up to an IV that has a lime green bag attached to it. They have a plastic bag covering it — I'm thinking because it's the color of toxin.

Let me recap yesterday: we got to the hospital around 10. I'm in the last room. It's nice. The nurses are sweet and the food isn't bad. Mom and I hung out for a while and then some people came by to see me. When Mr. Knox (a longtime friend whose kids went to school with Matt and me) saw me, he started crying. I know so many parents are so thankful it's not their kid and at the same time sympathize for my mom and dad.

I slept good through the night. Dad — poor guy — snores so loud. I usually don't wake up when I sleep, but, geeze, he is loud.

I started my first bag of chemo Friday at about 7:30. It's a 24-hour drip. Moving on to Saturday. Had a spinal tap this morning. It didn't hurt that bad. He numbed it up and I really didn't feel anything. That was #3. I'm getting flushed right now and will get a little bag of chemo in a few hours. I had a good day. My energy was good and I feel good. I'm going to be peeing all night. Neat.

March ??:

OK…not sure what day it is. I am thinking it's March 19. I'm feeling better today, but definitely not 100%. Last night and day was hell. I haven't been able to eat much. My appetite is getting better, but the thought of sitting down to a

3-course meal kinda makes me gag. Yesterday, I threw up 2 times and I had to use this cooling blanket. My fever reached 103.8°, so they put the blanket under me that generates the programmed temperature. Hello, 60 degrees! Good gosh, it was cold. They gave me this anti-nausea medicine—good call—AFTER I puked. Anywho, that...I forgot what I was going to say. DAMN. I've been here since Friday, March 15. I would be home if I didn't have this fever. They are checking for infection, but the nurses think it's the chemo. As of now, my mouth tastes like crap and I'm usually cold. And, my brain sucks.

I'm so excited for Meggan to be here.

March 20:

I feel so much better. I think I'm almost at 100%. This would be a perfect day if I had not started my frikin' period. Really could have done without that. I took a shower last night for the first time since I checked in here. Oops. Next time I will shower on the first or second day because by day three I usually feel like ass. I don't know why I said usually— like this is a normal thing for me.

So, I slept pretty good through the night—minus Dad's snoring. Around 3 a.m., the milk of magnesia kicked in. Harry from Dumb and Dumber. Well, at least I'm not constipated.

Oh, let me go back to the shower. First, you lose all modesty when you're in the hospital. I would feel totally comfortable being butt-naked and walking down the hall. I could care less. OK, Sybil, my nurse last night, is one of my favorites. She is an aggressive, no-nonsense type of lady. I like that about her, but she doesn't have to be that way when she is drying me off. I thought my skin was going to flake off she was rubbing so hard. Hey, lady, have you ever heard of dabbing? Easy, Tiger. Well, I felt better—but I was checking my legs for blood.

OK, so it's 4:05 on March 20th and I feel so good. How can I feel so good when I have cancer? Why is chemo so potent? It really sucks. So, how am I feeling about this cancer stuff? Honestly, it can kiss my ass. What the hell? Why is there cancer? Leukemia? Anything that affects people minding their own damn business? I don't understand. Those 3 days of throwing up and not eating really sucked. I can't imagine people going through this without support and without people praying for them. Last thing, I can't get over how bad I smell. It's horrible. 7th grade smelly kid with no idea about hygiene. That's me. I'm that kid. I need to take care of that.

So, the deal is to feel great through the night and go home tomorrow. Please—I really want to go home.

March 21:

Meggan arrives today at 9 o'clock. I'm so excited. Last time I saw that girl was in August. We usually try to see each other every 4 months or so. I'm glad I could make things work out and get her butt to Texas. She'll probably get here around 10:30.

Yesterday ended perfectly. Sarah came by and we chatted for a while. Kim called. Then, I called Tracy and I got a chance to talk to all of the girls. It was great.

Today I have to get blood—probably because the nurses draw blood by the pints. Geeze. It's so beautiful outside. I think Dad and I might go for a walk or maybe we'll just sit outside. I feel wonderful today. It's awesome. I feel so good. I told Mom last night, "I love life." I do. I love my family. I love my friends. I love living.

I was so close to dying it was scary. Gramps said the

amount of fluid around my heart was dangerous because the heart can't expand and fill up with blood if too much fluid is around it. If it can't fill up, it can't pump any blood out. Not good. Dr. Deur said my airway was the size of a string. Thank you, Lord. I know you want me here to do some things. I will. I will do special, special things for many people.

Hello again—same day—different person. Definitely high. They just gave me decadron and benadryl. That combo equals floatiness for Meg. I wish I had some profound ideas I could ramble on about, but I don't. I believe I'll just take a nap. Good call.

It's almost midnight. I'm about to get some sleepy-sleepy medicine. Meggan just left. I am so happy. She looks great and I'm just so glad she is here.

I weighed 137 today. That's good. I thought I would have dropped more weight after this round. Tomorrow I have the spinal tap in the morning and it would be awesome if I could leave tomorrow. But the infectious disease guy said probably Saturday. I talked to Randa and Katie tonight, too. It was great.

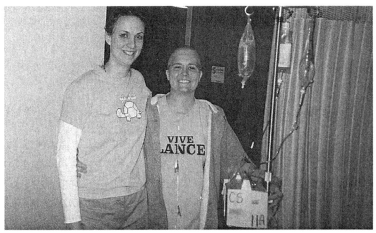

Meggan and Meg back from a walk

47

Bride Meggan and Bridesmaid Meg, July 2005

March 22:

Today I had another spinal tap. This time the needle hit a nerve and a shock shot down my leg. Twice. It felt so weird. Then, I turned over and immediately experienced the worst headache of my life. They gave me some drugs and I was out for 3 hours. Good Sleep. Meggan has been chillin' with me all day. No other visitors. It's been so perfect. We have taken a few walks and just had a great time. Hopefully, I'll be released tomorrow. I haven't had a fever in 3 days. It's time for me to say Peace Out.

March 25:

Today, I'm anemic. Yessss. I took a 4-hour nap and feel nothing. No more energy than before the nap. Right now, I'm experiencing a lovely headache as well as some diarrhea. It's wonderful.

March 26:

I went to the doctor's office this morning and I am so excited. I get to have a platelet transfusion tomorrow. Yes!

March 27:

What a splendid day! Today is the 23rd birthday. Didn't really think I would be in this spot on this day. Got some platelets to go along with my ice cream. Didn't take long— just a pain in the ass.

So many friends called today. They are so good to me. My friends, family, and people are medicine. Laughing is so good for the soul. It was a really good day. Tomorrow, I go in for another blood count. The counts should be good.

Dad and I walked around the neighborhood tonight. Didn't get too tired. It just amazes me that it's 10:15 and I feel like it is 3 in the morning. Tomorrow night, I'm venturing out of the house. Crazy me. Going over to Mary Ann's for dinner. I'm excited. Until tomorrow….

March 31:

Oh, what a wonderful weekend! Went to the country place (our family getaway for peace and quiet). Just the family. It was perfect. Slept a lot and played dominoes with Matt the rest of the time. Good gosh, he is funny. Such a good guy. I feel great today. My body is just sore. Other than that, I feel awesome. I want to talk more about my deeper thoughts, but I am not in the mood right now. Oh, read Bridget Jones's Diary this weekend. So funny. I think I laughed or smiled on every page. Lara and Erin came over today. We laughed almost the whole time they were here. It was so fun. Until deeper thoughts…

April 1:

Felt awesome today. I think it was from overflowing happiness from Erin's and Lara's visit. We had such a good time. They were here for 5 hours and it felt like 15 minutes. I'm fading. Note to self—start writing before midnight.

BRENDA and I played summer basketball together. She had just finished her last year of eligibility at Abilene Christian University when she heard I was sick. Since Brenda had graduated in December, she left school and came to Austin because she knew my family and I needed help. And she came through for us big time. She would bring stuff I wanted from the apartment to the hospital. She would run errands, such as getting hand lotion because everyone had to wash their hands every time they went out of the room and came back in. We counted on Brenda to see what needed doing. She was at the hospital every day in Austin. She brought me food. She stayed with me when I wanted someone in the room. She helped my dad pack up the apartment, and she drove my car home. She is the definition of a friend. Brenda would do anything for me.

MEGGAN K. played volleyball at The University. One of the reasons why I first loved talking to Meggan was because she was from Iowa. I loved hearing her talk because half the time I couldn't understand her. Ruff—no it's a roof. Crick—no it's a creek. Seriously, who is this girl? Meggan and I became very close friends and to this day she is one of my best friends. Just about every summer since freshman year, I have visited her wonderful family in Dubuque, Iowa. Because of Meggan, I got to meet more volleyball people. She introduced me to Mitra and all of Mitra's friends. When I got sick, Meggan was in school in Wisconsin. She flew down during her spring break to be with me in Arlington. Meggan would do anything for me.

MITRA played volleyball at UT and graduated a few years before me. Shortly after I came home to Arlington, Mitra moved to nearby Fort Worth to attend medical school. I enjoyed talking to Mitra about my treatment because unlike my non-medical school friends she actually knew what the heck I was talking about when I discussed a chemotherapy drug, a pill, or a side effect. Mitra is a dear friend. Mitra would do anything for me.

SARAH was my basketball teammate and friend in high school. She hit the three-point shot with no time left that forced overtime in the district championship game our senior year. We won in overtime (but that's not why I love her). She lived in Dallas when she heard the news I was sick. As soon as she got word, she headed to Austin. She drove three hours one way to see me for five minutes. Sarah always called, always cared, and always prayed for me. Sarah, along with her roommate Kat, ran the White Rock marathon in my honor and raised money for The Leukemia & Lymphoma Society in December 2002. Sarah would do anything for me.

KIM and I were teammates for two years in college. She was the leader and she took me in as a freshman. I loved being around Kim because she made me laugh. We have a similar sense of humor. It's always a plus when your friends get your jokes. Kim is loyal, honest, and funny—so funny I have to mention it twice. When Kim took a coaching job in Irvine, California, she became my California connection. I took one trip out there before I got sick and two more after I was into my recovery. Kim would do anything for me.

Meg and Randa, senior year

RANDA was a teammate in college and was also an education major. When basketball was over for us, we still saw each other all the time since we were in the same classes. It was like we were twelve years old again. We were so excited to be sitting next to each other, not listening, writing notes, and asking our classmates, "What are we supposed to be doing?" Randa and I shared a bond through basketball because most of the time you would find us near the water. For you non-athletes, being by the water means you probably aren't going to get to play much. We were buddies. It was guaranteed: every time I went in the game, Randa was my biggest fan. Randa would do anything for me.

MARY ANN is a year older than me. We met on the soccer field when we were in elementary school. We became good friends in high school. Since Mary Ann would always take care of everybody, she was known as the "mom." If people needed to talk, Mary Ann would listen and figure out a way to try to make things better. When Mary Ann would come to visit me, I loved it for three reasons. First, she always brought me food. Whether it was a milkshake or quesadillas, she went out and got what I was in the mood for. Second, she is so comfortable. If I wasn't feeling well, she would just rub my head or she recognized that it wasn't a good time and she would leave. Third, she gives the best foot massages ever. Besides that, she would give me great pedicures. My face might have been huge; I might have just puked for the third time; my head could have been pounding, but I guarantee you, my toenails always looked good. To this day and for always, Mary Ann and the entire Starns family are special, special people who will always have a place in my heart. Mary Ann would do anything for me.

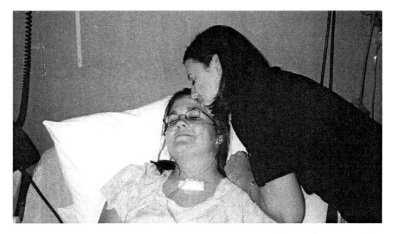

Andrea and Meg in ICU

ANDREA is Mary Ann's sister. She is two years younger than me. She played soccer at Texas A&M University. Andrea was one of the first ones I remember seeing in ICU. This was the scene: She is crying. I've got tubes everywhere with the puke bucket to my left and the bed pan to my right. She says something like, "I didn't believe it when my dad told me you had cancer." I told her she probably said to her dad, "What? Meg is dating a guy named Lancer? Huh? What? Omigosh, she has cancer?. *&^%!" I remember that because it was the first time I laughed in ICU. From then on, we called the tumor Lancer.

Andrea has always loved me. In that district championship game for Arlington High in 1997, she wrote on her arm, MEG IS MY HERO. She got in the newspaper for that. I could always laugh with Andrea. Andrea would do anything for me.

ERIN was a swimmer at UT. She lived two floors down from me in the dorm. Erin and I finished our eligibility at the same time. Once we "retired," there always seemed to be a party around Erin. When I was in the hospital in Austin, she called every morning to see if I wanted some non-hospital breakfast food. She brought my dad breakfast, too. Even if I was indecisive about breakfast (because of my lack of appetite), she brought some anyway. Secretly, I think Dad enjoyed her visits just as much as I did.☺ Erin is good to all of her friends. In fact, her nickname is Best Friend. Erin would do anything for me.

(On April 29, 2008, Erin was diagnosed with Stage II Nodular Sclerosis Hodgkin's Disease. She currently lives in California and is undergoing chemotherapy treatments. Unbelievable. Two college athletes. Two friends. Two young women learning about perspective before age 30. Like me, Erin's friends would do anything for her.)

Chapter 8   Survival Secrets: Love

In the spring of 2003, as I began speaking to church groups, sports teams, and service organizations, I realized I did more than just relate what happened to me. I shared valuable lessons—lessons for life—which I learned as a patient and a cancer survivor fighting my way back to health. Because I had known so many people with cancer who did not make it, I started to ask questions:

"Why am I here?"

"Did I do anything differently from my friends who passed?"

Looking back, I recognize six factors helped me survive. These factors can help anyone who is struggling—not just someone fighting cancer.

My survival secrets:

· love
· positive attitude
· medicine (including doctors, nurses and scientific advances)
· faith
· exercise
· luck

All of these factors together saved my life. I would not have made it if even one had been missing. I have to start with the factor that never failed me.

For whatever reason, I have a lot of love in my soul. I don't know if I am just one of those blessed people who loves to love others, or if being around love all my life makes it a natural feeling.

During the cancer times, love was one of the reasons why I got up every morning. I loved my life. I loved the people in my life. They loved me. I cannot remember one day of my illness passing without being told, "I love you." I heard it from my parents, my brother, my family, my best friends, my parents' friends, teachers, coaches, ministers, and strangers. Receiving letters, emails, phone calls, and visits instantly lifted my spirits. It didn't matter if I felt better for just five minutes because, I promise you, those were the best five minutes of the day.

When drugs could not take away the pain in my stomach, joints, or head, I would envision thousands of hands placed on my body. From these hands, light would emanate. This light represented love. These were the hands of my family, my friends, my nurses, the hands of God, and even of strangers. Even though all of these hands didn't know each other, they were bound by one thing—love for me. And all of these hands wanted me to get better.

During a time of weakness and vulnerability, knowing that so many people were praying for me, thinking about me, and loving me gave me a sense of invincibility. Obviously, I wasn't invincible since I was bald and lying in the hospital bed, but the love gave me strength. It gave me courage and energy and determination.

Because I love my family so much, I fought like hell for things to be back to normal for us. Because I love my friends so much, I thought about all of the good times we had had and the good times ahead—when I was better. Because I love my life so much, I didn't want to leave it. I didn't want to die because I love being here.

The love in my life and the love in my heart gave me an advantage to fight the disease. Without the love, the days would have been longer, fun times between treatments would not have happened, and I don't think I would be here today.

Chapter 9   April 2 – April 30, 2002

April 2:
    I got a great letter from Martha today. She sounds good and strong. She wants us to get through these times together. I think she is faced with a tougher challenge. I don't depend on anything. She has to break some intense habits. I just have to get treatment and take naps. I think we will have fun hearing each other's stories.

April 4:
    Oh, and we are back at the hospital. Gotta love it. I'm so bloated from drinking a liter of this stuff for a CT scan. This stuff highlights the tumors and cancer cells. That combined with a bag of glucose makes me pee about every hour. I've already finished one bag of cytoxan—I really wish they would pick another name for that. Nothing like knowing you are putting something into your body

Ready for Round 4

that means "Cell-Killer." Mom asked me today how I felt about things. I told her I really didn't feel anything. I just know I have a job to do and it's time to do it. I don't have many options. It's either do the chemo or die. Not too excited about the second one.

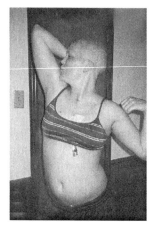

HUGH HEFNER, CALL ME!

April 6:

What does cancer feel like?

Fatigue, weakness, but strength at the same time. I say strength because I know I'm beating it. Here is this dangerous, murderous foreign mass inside my body trying to kill me. That is what is so scary. This mutation wants to kill me. I have been "lucky" because I have not been hovering over the toilet, puking my brains out. I've gotten sick a few times, but no extensive pain.

What does cancer do to the mind? First of all, I have trouble remembering things. My vocabulary seems to be quite limited. The simplest things I forget. Thank goodness, I'm not 75 and dealing with this. My body is young, strong, and can fight this off. Cancer puts things in perspective. Really, what is important? Your clothes? Your looks? Hell, NO! Your future? To a degree. We all have plans, but do they really matter? The next hour in the day has become my future. People have asked me what I'm going to do and that's a little hard to think about in the hospital, tied to an IV pole, and wondering if I should eat 2 crackers or 3. What would I like to make of this whole adventure? I would like to speak to young kids about challenges, decision making, college experience, and, of course, cancer. I want people to see that I'm living a good life with cancer. Cancer does not mean a death sentence. I really want to share my story—either on paper or in person—sharing it with Oprah would be cool. Everybody wants to get on Oprah. I just want people to see how Mom and I end up getting through this.

April 10:
Oh, for the love…I love chemo…really I do. I love how I have sat through this entire day feeling my stomach rumble and pass gas. I love how I feel this inner heat from somewhere so deep it only escapes through my head. I love how taking a shower compares to a marathon. I love that I can't feel this pen in my hand. I love that I feel like I have been folded up inside a very small box. Oh, chemo…I love you so much. You make me forget and you make me ask the dumbest questions ever. I'm just glad you are a part of my life.
*Overall, the round went well. Did not puke. Praise the Lord. No fever. Only fell once—not hard. I took a shower. Did not get constipated. Yea for me. I did have this one type of chemo called adriamycin or something and it's a **bitch**. Right now, it just feels like I have 10 pounds of cement in my stomach. Excuse me here, but I think I crapped out most of that medicine this morning. Not kidding—at least 10 pounds of crap. Sorry.*
Good news—Mom had another checkup today and is still cancer free. Her counts are almost normal. Yahoo! Like she says every day, SHE IS CANCER FREE.
Good news—My tumor is 90% gone. Holy Cow! That is awesome. It was measuring 2.5 cm by 5 cm before round 3. Before I started chemo, it was 18 cm across—that's 7.5

inches. Yikes! My mom asked Dr. Deur about my string size airway today. He said that if I had been drinking water and it had gone down the wrong pipe, that would have been it. He said the only reason I survived the amount of time with the symptoms I had was because I was in such good cardiovascular condition.

*I'm pretty pumped about the tumor shrinking, but it's what I expected. I didn't know, however, it would shrink that fast. But I never really thought I was going anywhere (heaven) with this thing. Again, the chemo helps. Visualization is a plus. Positive attitude is a must. But those **prayers** are amazing. Why are people in London praying for me? Because there are so many good people. People who don't know me are asking about me. They are taking the time out of their day to say my name and lift me up. It's quite unbelievable when I really think about it.*

April 23:

I went to Austin for the weekend and had such a great time. I got to see so many of my friends. About 15 of us went out to eat at Hula Hut and laughed most of the evening. I loved every minute of it. Now I'm back at the doctor's office and waiting. I think I've gained a few pounds. Getting my belly back. Tomorrow is round 4. Halfway.

April 29:

OK, round 4 is almost over. Almost over means I'm almost out of the hospital. This round can kiss my ass. First of all, I look like total crap. I don't understand—why must I have acne? I lose my hair in ALL places, my modesty, my tonsils, my memory, and now I have acne. This round, let's see, what happened? Oh, fever, ice packs, fever 103.8°, cooling blanket…Shit. I hate that damn thing. Nothing like laying or lying (never understood that rule) on a 60 degree blanket for two and a half friggin' hours. I've got bed sores from taking an 8 hour nap—which I don't think you can call a nap—a rash all over, swollen ankles—it hurts like hell to walk—and emotional trauma. It's not fun when walking is a bitch. My heels and ankles are so incredibly tight. Yeah, on Saturday, I'm going to say one of the worst (maybe **the** worst) pains of my life. Damn that pain.

I'm physically starting to feel better, but it's been an emotional day from hell. April 29, 2002 can kiss my ass. Holy Cow, it sucked. First, I find out that Emily Hunter came out of remission. Geeze. She is only 15. She has bone cancer and was finally able to go back to school, but only for a month. What the hell? She goes through all of that chemo, starts to feel good about life and herself, and she has to go back to the hospital and go through it again. And those stories are ones you just don't want to hear.

Then, I told Mom about Grady. (Grady was a grade school through high school classmate who was diagnosed with testicular cancer about the same time I got my lymphoma news.) I visited his room last night. He looks nothing like I expected him to look. He couldn't really talk. I don't know if he just felt so bad or it was the pain killers, but that was not fun seeing him.

Around 2:30 this afternoon, I got up to go for a walk. I walked by the nurses station and we were joking around. HA! HA! Good times had by all. As I walked down the hall, I saw a man in some type of uniform walk into the last room on the right. I had a weird feeling as he passed me. Out from that room came a bed, but the sheets were not their normal white. They were navy blue. These navy blue sheets covered the body of someone who had just passed away. The man in the uniform was taking the body down to the morgue. We exchanged looks in the hallway and the tears started flowing. I never imagined I would be that close to death. I turned around and my nurse came over to see if I was OK. Not so much. Started crying. No. More like bawling. Aunt Beth, my mom's sister, was here. She was such a comfort and I'm glad she was here. My dad came out about 3. He was here when a friend of the patient in the room next to me went out into the hall and started screaming. The one time my door was open…damn.

Later, Chet (my classmate who I kinda had a crush on since 2nd grade), Denver (a classmate of Matt's), and Brenda came by. Brenda was here when that woman next door passed away. The woman was in her 40s. I knew exactly when it happened because her visitors started wailing. The nurses said that the relatives were not accepting her death. Yeah, not a good day. Two people died on my floor of a disease I've got. I'm not even thinking about that option for me, but it's just that I forget or I want to forget that some people don't do well. So to say the least, not my best day emotionally.

I have decided my new thing to say is LIVE EACH DAY. That's what I feel. People need to do that. It's easier that way. I was so close to dying. I want to live. I want to hear the birds. I want to smile and make people smile. Anywho—a big day. One I wish was filled with happier moments. I am hoping to go home tomorrow, but if not, what's another bed sore.

April 30:

"The radiologist looked at the chest x-ray and he said it shows no sign of disease." —Dr. Deur.

I asked him if that means NO TUMOR and he said ALMOST. Holy Cow…My tumor is almost gone. If there are no cells in the bone marrow, I will be in remission. What a great day.

MARTHA and I met each other playing select soccer when I was in sixth grade and Martha was in fifth. Martha was one of the best soccer players I had ever seen. The first time I met Martha, I knew in an instant we were going to be friends. She had a short boyish haircut like mine instead of the standard pony tail or braids. We had the same interests; we had the same sense of humor, and we were great teammates for each other.

Martha & Meg, 1992

After I quit playing soccer to concentrate on basketball, Martha and I didn't see each other much. We didn't live in the same town or go to the same school. Our lives went in different directions—in more ways than one— when we reached high school.

Martha developed a sickness of her own. Her sickness was addiction. At the time I got sick, Martha was in a rehabilitation center in the Northeast. She knew I was sick, and I knew she was sick. Because she could not receive phone calls or emails, we could only communicate through letters. Writing to Martha was part of my therapy. We would both write about the good, innocent times of the past, the not-so-great times of the present, and how bright and worthwhile the future would be. I would laugh out loud reading her letters, and I know she did the same. Although we were both restricted and limited during this time in our lives, we did all we could for each other.

63

May 2:

Yesterday, I saw Grady and he didn't look so good. His eyes looked defeated. I don't know how I would look if I had 30 mouth sores. He couldn't eat or drink and could barely talk. I'm scared for Grady. He should be going home soon, but I think he has to go right back in.

May 6:

Hello, Fatigue. 3rd day in a row I have taken a 2 hour nap and could have gone for more. But I'm excited for the first time in my life to have my period. I think it would be a good idea for that little cycle to continue. I'd really like all my organs down there to keep working.

May 8:

Cancer Sucks. I'm quite bored with it really. Today, my counts suck. I have to go in for a blood transfusion tomorrow. Cancer just controls everything. I shouldn't be around people because of infection. I can't go outside because it's hotter than hell and my skin will fry. Don't make plans because if the counts aren't good, plans are cancelled. Yes, today was officially my depressed day. Sometimes I still can't believe I have cancer. I feel like I'm living another life… it's kinda hard to explain. I'm off to walk very slowly on the treadmill.

May 9:

Damn, I still have cancer. These past few days have been rough. I know it will be over soon and we'll look back and say, "That went by so fast." Yeah—well, it sucks right now.

I feel like I do nothing during the day. Por ejemplo, today I was at the hospital from 8:30 – 12:30, came home, ate lunch. I read and napped until dinner, and then watched TV the rest of the night. It seems like I do nothing. I don't know what I think I should be doing, but I am really getting bored. The days seem to go by so fast sometimes. How can they go by fast when I do nothing? I want to do something…I don't know what, but something. I'm starting to really miss people. I miss my friends. At first, it wasn't bad because people were coming by here and the attitude of YOU GOTTA DO WHAT YOU GOTTA DO was still fresh on the mind. I still have that attitude…it's just that I want to do something else.

It's hard to do stuff because of the chances of getting sick. You want to do stuff, but you can't. It's almost midnight and I'm wondering, "How in the hell did this happen? Have I really been in Arlington for 3 months? Did I really leave all of my friends because I was sick?" It feels like a movie. Sometimes I just get scared. I know anything can happen. I know car accidents can happen, plane crashes, September 11…I know all of this stuff. I just don't want it to happen.

A family in Austin today was driving their pregnant 18-year-old daughter to the hospital for her delivery. They had a head on collision. The drivers of both cars die. The daughter, her child, and three other passengers die. Why? Why them? Crap like that I just don't understand. BARF! I really don't like thinking about these things. Quite depressing.

OK, tomorrow is a new day with new beginnings. Until later…

May 13:

I'm feeling better emotionally and physically. I still have cancer, which is disappointing, but my spirits are better and that always helps. I think I have been so tired with everything because my body has reached toxicity according to Dr. Deur. I've been taking 2 hour naps just about every day.

Sunday, Mom and I went to church while the pagan boys (Matt and Dad) stayed at home. Sunday was Mother's Day. This day is kinda overdone. Mothers are indeed special. No doubt about mine. But what about the mothers who aren't or who have moved on to heaven? So, the sermon was good for me, but it could have been depressing for those who didn't have good mothers or who have none at all.

Meg at her Graduation Party

May 16 - May 19:

Well, I'm back in Austin. I love this place. I love this town and LOVE seeing all of my friends. Thursday, we all met up at Trudy's, my favorite hangout. The chemo has definitely helped the tolerance. I don't really feel much when I drink. The Mexican Martinis are still oh-so-good. Saturday was my big GRADUATION DAY. It was a great ceremony and it was so cool seeing all of my buddies in their caps and gowns. After the ceremony, we went to Serrano's for my graduation celebration. So many people came by—from high school buddies, to athletes, to academic counselors, professors, coaches, and my dearest friends. It was a wonderful weekend. I will never forget it.

I go in tomorrow for Round 5. I'm getting closer. I think there are about 2½ months left. I can do that.

Paul (Gramps), Cathy (Mom), Matt (brother), Meg, Zora (Gram), Ron (Dad) on Graduation Day, Austin, Texas

May 21:

Round 5—how the heck are ya? I'm doing splendid, thank you. I checked in today at 5' 9" and 142 pounds. My blood pressure was 100/60. Healthy as a horse. Mom and I are watching Days of Our Lives. Hanging out. Waiting on the goods.

As a basketball player, as a friend, as a person, as a cancer patient, I have always seen the glass half-full. When you are fighting for your life, you can't afford to be negative. You can't waste energy on thinking about how crappy this whole thing is. It's crappy—that's all there is to it, but what are you going to do to make it less crappy? Cancer sucks—absolutely. But if you can find some humor in the whole thing, it is manageable.

So I laughed. Laughing got me through the day. Laughing made me forget I was bald, had a cord sticking out of my boob, and had just thrown up. Laughing forces you to be positive. Laughing is an expression of joy and having joy in your heart makes you positive. I remember one time when I was going out with some girlfriends and I decided being bald can be cute. I took a shower for the first time in a few days; washed and shined my head; put on some make-up; put on these big hoop earrings; wrapped my head up in a bandana; went to the mirror to see how cute I was—and I looked like pirate. I promise—a pirate.

Now really, what could I do? I could get mad, depressed and upset, or I could be happy I was going out with my friends. I could be happy I was alive. I could laugh because in an effort to be sassy, I looked like a cartoon character.

Cancer strips you of your physical appearance, your physical strength, your modesty, your energy, and just about everything else. It doesn't have to strip you of your attitude. It doesn't have to strip you of your sense of humor. You can still see the glass half-full, and you can still have fun being bald looking like a pirate.

Chapter 12   May 23 – June 10, 2002

May 23:

Day 3 in the hospital. I've had 4 bags of cytoxan. I'm a little tired and a little nauseated. But other than that, I'm OK. Yesterday was a good visitor day. I don't want to jinx myself, but I'm doing all right. I've started to think about life after cancer. There is something about being done with each round. There is hope and light. I know I shouldn't think about it as much as I do, but I DON'T WANT A BONE MARROW TRANSPLANT. I really think I'm in remission. Oh, did I mention the spinal tap was a little painful? I don't think the doctor on call for Dr. Deur drew out the fluid where he numbed it. Damn. I could have done without feeling every poke and burn. Definitely.

May 27:

It's Memorial Day. Round 5 is over—kind of. I've got that last spinal tap and a little push (a syringeful) of vincristine. I don't know if I'm getting used to the chemo or if I'm getting better, but it seems to be getting easier. Mom said once you are over that halfway hump, things change. So true. I don't know why, but I feel like I'm almost done. This round, I did not get sick. I just felt like ass for a couple of days and that was not even that bad. Knock on wood.

Last night, Mom and I watched a memoriam for September 11. How in the hell did that happen? Watching it last night was the first time I saw bodies falling from the building. It was awful. "Awful" does not give it justice. I could not even imagine being there, losing somebody, or being even remotely close to the whole thing. It makes me sick to think about it.

Today is another chill day. Shocker. I'm still feeling a little queasy and I find myself going to the bathroom quite frequently. Very soon I'll be writing pages upon pages of intellectual insight. I just don't know when.

Hello again…probably the longest day of my life. I guess that's what happens when you sit on your ass all day. It seems like I was in the hospital weeks ago. No, that would be yesterday.

My stomach is a little unsettled at this moment. I'll be rocking the house here soon and it's not going to be pretty.

The news was awful today. A bridge collapsed in Oklahoma yesterday. They have no idea the number of victims. A bus wrecked and killed someone. 4 people were killed here the other day and 4 others in Austin. Watched a segment on war veterans. Horrible. Depressing. No wonder people have problems. We need to have a National Day of Good News. No one can report anything bad. Oh, another suicide bomber. Killed an 18-month-old baby. What the hell is the point?

I feel big thoughts coming, but I also feel sleep. I'll pick this up tomorrow.

Yes, my stomach is fighting itself. What a pleasant feeling. Oh, Dad is afraid I'm getting bored. He is so right. I'm terribly bored. I'm supposed to keep my mind active which is quite hard to do when that used to mean physical activity. I've read books—I'm going to have to put a halt on the cancer ones. I really wish I'd learn sign language. Really want to get on that. I'm off to drink some fluids so my bowels will move. That's a sentence I never thought I would say. Oh the pleasures…until tomorrow.

June 2:

It's been a while. Tuesday I hung out with Mary Ann

and Andrea all day. We went to Pappadeaux that night. Good times. Thursday, I went to a bachelorette party for Megan C., a high school friend. We went to the Fish Bowl to eat and back to her house to open some panty presents (don't know how to spell 'lawnzheray'). Later, a few of the girls went to HAVE A NICE DAY CAFÉ. So fun. It was all '70s and '80s music with a little bit of today's hip-hop. I wore jeans and my I WANT YOUR BODY t-shirt with some sweet, pimp-looking glasses. I did not move as swift as usual, but I had such a great time. I was thinking, "It's so great to be alive. Thank you, Lord."

Friday, I had a spinal tap. Not bad. My blood counts were not too low, but I am wondering if I might have to have a transfusion soon. Whatever.

Meg and Mary Ann heading to the bachelorette party.

Meg and Megan C.
at Have A Nice Day Café

June 4:

Yesterday was quite busy. I finished reading Siegel's book on Love, Medicine, and Miracles. He suggested when jounaling to record feelings rather than events. That's a good call, since I seem to have trouble remembering events. I'll try to do both.

I went to the doctor and it took a little longer because they didn't have my records. Convenient. I went to the mall to try and get some cute shirts. I think I got a few good ones. I got a pretty good walking workout. My legs are sore today. I don't know if that's from walking or from the shots. Whatever.

What was kind of cool about yesterday was this vendor guy was almost flirting with me. I don't know if he does that with everyone or if he felt sorry for me, but it was fun. He asked me to sit down and take a load off, but I declined. Didn't want to fall asleep on him. It was nice to be offered, though.

In Bernie Siegel's book, the big theme is Love. You have

to love yourself as well as others. There is no reason for enemies. It's a waste of time. Open your heart to all and healing will prevail. I really enjoyed the book. It made sense to me that in order to heal, you have to take care of yourself and not just let things happen.

People have asked me what is next, and I have absolutely no idea. What I would love to do is work with kids at camp for the rest of my life. I don't know if that would be a sports camp or a camp for kids with cancer.

But the first thing I'll do is visit all of my friends on my Victory Tour—Boston, NYC, Madison, Dubuque, Colorado, Ohio, Seattle, California, and Mom wants to hit Australia. I don't know how I can afford all that, but it'll be fun trying.

OK, until next time. Oh, my legs…

June 5:

For the love of the Lord! Last night…sucked. Quite a bit of pain in the legs. Holy cow, it friggin' hurt. It was a combination of withdrawal from coming off the steroids and big shots of neupegen. Mom slept with me—love that lady—and we stayed up most of the night. I think I slept about 2 hours. Oh, well…I'm not hurting right now, so things are better. It's nap time.

(Neupegen shots stimulate the bone marrow to produce white blood cells. When cancer patients' white counts drop to nearly zero, the infection fighting mechanism is gone. Because that puts them at high risk for infection, the patients get neupegen shots, usually three shots over five days. As the bone marrow cranks up to make more cells, the bones ache. It's as if the marrow has gotten too big for the bones and the bones are being pressured to expand—which they can't.)

June 7:

Helloooooo! I'm in Austin. I love hanging with my buddies. I got in yesterday around 2. Aunt Barbara picked me up in Waco. Too sweet. After a nap, I went out to eat with Tracy, Randa, Katie, and Dawn. Hey, Fat Girls. It's kinda nice to not really care what you eat because food is just so good. I know I'm gaining weight, but does it really matter? No, not so much. Aunt Flo (the dreaded cycle) is in town. She is so annoying. She makes me feel huge, a little moody, and now I have to worry about platelets. Geeze!!

June 10:

I had an absolute blast this weekend at Katie's bachelorette party. We hit a few bars and ended up at Ivory Cat which is a great piano bar. I always have so much fun when we go there. I don't think I have ever laughed so much in a 24 hour period. People were drunk, but not too drunk. It was great. Sunday, I could barely walk. My ankles were swollen and extremely tight. I'm pretty sure it's from walking all over Austin. Oh well, I wouldn't trade it.

Today I'm back in the hospital. Round 6 is underway. I had the bone marrow biopsy this morning. The numbing stick burned. There was pressure and I could feel him pulling something out. It's just weird to think, "Hey, he's touching my bone." This round is a big one. I'll find out a lot of stuff this round. I'm feeling REMISSION. Sarah came up to visit today. Always have fun chattin' with her.

My plan for this round is to read 3 books. Yeah, right. OK, I'm about to start chemo in 30 minutes. I'm so excited.

Chapter 13   June 15 – June 27, 2002

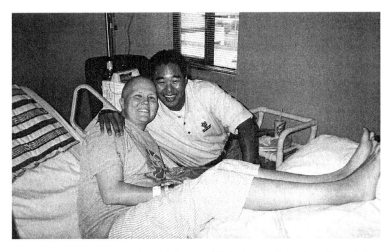

Meg, Blake, and Meg's swollen, discolored feet

June 15:

What a week! It started on Tuesday morning with a fever. Usually with this round, I get a fever on the third or fourth day. Not so much. This time the fever came about 8 hours after I started the chemo. Anywho, Wednesday sucked. I woke up with a fever of 101° something. Got my spinal tap done. Dr. Deur came in and said **MY TUMOR IS GONE**. That was great, but we headed downhill after that. I'm just going to sum up the week. My fever lasted from Tuesday to Friday. On Friday, it reached 105.8°. Little hot. Damn. I had ice packs everywhere—armpits, groin, stomach. I put one under my head as a pillow, but the nurse didn't think that was a good idea. I was on the cooling blanket for 2 straight days. It stunk because I had the chills and then to be put on a blanket at 60 degrees is pure hell. My groshong got infected and they took it out on Friday. I'll get a new one Monday.

Currently, my ankles are quite swollen and red.

A highlight of the week was Blake came over on Thursday. It was good timing. I didn't feel too bad when he was here, but he had to leave because I started to get the chills again. I think I scared him. The thing about these chills is they aren't just BRRRR, I'M COLD CHILLS. No, No. You are freezing and you shake so violently. It's a good workout, but I would rather build strength another way.

Now, we are just waiting on the biopsy for me to say that I'm in Remission. I want to say that. I want to feel victorious. I want this shit to be over. It is so tiresome. I always feel like I can get back up, but sometimes it gets harder and harder. I'm so ready to start my life again. Even though I'll be in Arlington, I'll be getting stronger and I'll be cancer free. Here's the catch…I still don't know if I have to do a bone marrow transplant. I'll find out in a week or so.

Mom went to Dallas today to listen to a rep from M.D. Anderson. The lady said radiation is probably in the future. Sonofa.

June 18:
I'M IN REMISSION. NO MORE CANCER!!! EVER!!!

Meg, Gram, Gramps

June 20:

Yesterday was rough. I was so tired. Matt came home and, boy, does he make me laugh. Dad took him to the airport to work a football camp for the Tampa Bay Bucs. I should have told him to get a picture with Mike Alstot—a cutie—no, a hottie. Yesterday was also the grandparents 59th wedding anniversary. During the midst of our celebration, who gets sick? That would be the bald kid. I couldn't eat dinner, had to be excused from the table, and go lie down. Dammit, it never leaves. As long as I'm doing this chemo thing, there are reminders everywhere I'm not normal. Por ejemplo—no hair, hot flashes, no fruits or veggies, always wondering if people have washed their hands, swollen ankles, frequent doctor visits, can't go out to eat or be in large crowds, transfusions, exert a little energy and need a 4-hour nap. The list goes on.

One thing that stinks is Yes, I'm in remission, but I don't feel any different. Maybe I don't because I have been so tired. I think the main thing is I'm in remission, but I still have a

79

lot of shit to do. As people keep telling me, "You're winning the battles, but you still have the war." That's true. I went into remission very quickly. I beat that fucking tumor. So if I'm winning, why doesn't it feel that way?

A couple of more things to bitch about. I think they put the groshong in the wrong place. It's not sore. It's uncomfortable when I move in certain directions. I'm hoping it will get better and they won't have to replace it or adjust it. Just a pain in the ass.

The other thing was my doctor's visit. It looks like my ass will be doing radiation. Son of a bitch. One of the nurses asked if I have saved my eggs. Uhhh…no. I couldn't in Austin because I was in such dire need of help. We didn't have time to go through the process of harvesting eggs. (Besides, we found out later that unfertilized eggs don't freeze well. I didn't happen to have any fertilized ones handy.) The nurse said I'll need to do that before the transplant because — I believe she said — "There is no way they'll survive." Great. Again, another bullshit side effect. What a bunch of shit! We shouldn't have to worry about this.

What is tough is explaining to my friends that even though I'm in remission, I'm not healthy. The old Meg is not back yet and won't be for a while. I tell them I still have stuff to do and they are so surprised. I don't like thinking about the What Ifs. It sucks that this comes back in some people. It sucks, in general, and I'm just tired of it. I think overall, I'm just tired. I'm tired of this routine. I'm tired of feeling tired. I'm tired of all of the things I listed before. I'm tired of being sick. I want to start my new life.

June 22:

I have not done much the past few days. My energy level has basically crashed and naps have been frequent. Yesterday,

I got my CBC (complete blood count) and my white blood count was 3, normal is between 5 and 10, and I had 8,000 platelets. Normal for platelets is between 150,000–400,000. Oops. Got a transfusion. The whole ordeal lasted about 5 hours. Why do I feel like I spend all of my time at the doctor's office or hospital?

Because my counts are so low and my recovery after this round has been slow, I will not be able to attend UT soccer player Jessica's wedding. Nothing ever seems normal. I hate to be an I CAN'T person, but that's what I feel like. I CAN'T get in big crowds. I CAN'T be in the heat. I CAN'T go over to someone's house who lives more than 10 minutes away. It's so much bull. Last night, Morgen came over for dinner and then we were going to go to a movie. Nope. Not good to be around too many people. Blah, blah, blah…

I think I'm going to try to talk to somebody who has gone through what I'm going through. That was Mom's suggestion. There is only so much understanding she can do and even less from my friends. You have to go through this to know what is going on. Por ejemplo, I thought about eating pancakes at IHOP. Yummy!! Yeah, sure can't because my white blood count is too low so I shouldn't eat in a restaurant. What a bunch of crap.

Mom spent some time on the internet last night looking up lymphoma and transplant stuff. I don't think she was too excited about what she read. The chemo is a bitch and I heard the recovery process is not the best. We go to Baylor University Medical Center in Dallas Wednesday. I'm hoping we will get enough information, so I'll be able to think about it and make a decision. I really would like the doctors to look at my slides and charts and say, "It really doesn't matter what you do. It's 50/50 either way." That would be so easy. I would say, "Hell, no, I'm not going to do it!" That would be so great now, wouldn't it? I really just want to have to do radiation and that's it. I want to be done with this thing. I want to appreciate life—which I think I do—but I want to get out and smell the flowers, feel the rain, listen to the birds, and not worry about frying my skin, touching people, passing out, and all of the other crap I think about.

This journal has been a wonderful release. Thank you, Erin, for this gift.

June 24:

Hellooooo. It's the start of a new journal. I've been feeling better the last few days. Naps are still frequent, but I'm not super tired and weak. Yesterday, I walked a mile. I felt so good afterward. My knees and ankles are cussing me, but it was fun. My ankles blistered from this last batch of chemo and when I took a shower, one of the blisters filled up with water. It was so nasty. Kinda cool when it popped, but still disgusting.

I talked to Ally the other day. It was so great talking to somebody who knows. It's so refreshing to talk to someone who appreciates life. It's not like my friends don't, but they have not been face to face with their own mortality. I think Lara comes the closest to understanding. Her 16-year-old cousin Laine died in a car accident Lara's junior year of college. I think Lara has always been a lover-of-life type person, but maybe after Laine died, she realized how short life can be.

Well, I'm off to the doctor's office. I will get a shot today. Hopefully, I'll have some bone pain because that means my counts are going up. I'll write more later...

Blood counts...not so good. Platelet count was down to 10,000. Dr. Deur wanted me to get my ankles checked and also see the groshong man. So, we went to the hospital to get platelets. 2 hours later…still no platelets. The reason I didn't get the platelets was because of a church bus crash. The kids were between 11- and 17-years-old. 5 people are dead and 36 injured. I really don't understand. Why do bad things happen? This bus crash was just one of several accidents that seem to have happened within the last month.

I'm cancer free today and every day for the rest of my life.

June 25:

I'm going to pick up where I left off yesterday. I just don't understand why all this bad stuff happens. I'm dealing with my own illness (do I still say illness even though I'm in remission?), but there are so many things that can "end it." I don't know if death scares me or if it's just I want to live. But there are so many carefree people and people with faith and so many of these people die. Why? This isn't a "Why Me" entry. This is a "why is there terrorism" entry? Why did 6 of 8 people in one family die in a car accident? Why was Elizabeth Smart kidnapped? It's a bunch of crap. People say that God never gives us anything we can't handle. I don't know if I like that one. I know that God is always with us and He comforts us in our time of need, but does He not "give" situations to some people because He knows they can't handle it? You either handle it or you don't. You get through it while others might have mental breakdowns, commit suicide, or live life in a funk. Oh blah…I get so annoyed when I think about bad stuff happening to my friends and family…Moving on…

I got some platelets and saw Grady. He looked great. He might just have one more treatment, maybe some surgery, and be done. That would be awesome.

My groshong is good to go. Naturally, I go to the doctor and everything is fine. It was not as red today or as sore. Oh well…

Tomorrow is the big day. It's the consultation at Baylor. I don't think I'm scared or nervous. I just want an end point. If I have to do the bone marrow transplant, that will absolutely suck and it can kiss my ass, but at least I'll know of a plan. If I just have to do radiation (Ah-hem…that would be nice), then I'll have an end date. I'm done for the night.

I'm cancer free today and every day for the rest of my life. Peace out.

June 26:

Holy Geeze! Information overload. I don't know how much of this I'm going to be able to do because I'm getting those bright migraine things. We just got back from the Bone Marrow Consult in Dallas. Damn. It lasted 3½ hours. We got a lot of information. Most of it I really didn't want to hear. This is what I got out of it. I was pretty damn sick. The doctor said I might have lasted another week. OK—not going to write anymore because those bright things are blinding. Until tomorrow…..

I'm cancer free today and every day for the rest of my life.

June 27:

OK, I'm back and no headaches. Let's talk about yesterday's meeting. Good people. Very organized. Had their act together. Dr. Berryman is a young guy and he talked to us for quite a while. This is what I got out of it: My cancer is the second most aggressive type of non-Hodgkins Lymphoma. He said that the chances of my cancer recurring are 40 - 50%. In my opinion, that sucks. He said there were 3 risk areas in which to consider a transplant. The first is the stage of the cancer. Mine was stage IV = HIGH RISK. The second is the patient's performance at the time of diagnosis. Since he told me I was about a week away from dying, I'm going to say my *performance would be poor = HIGH RISK. The third is the LDH. I have no idea what that means. I think tumor activity. Dr. Berryman said it was high = HIGH RISK. So, I'm batting 1000 here. But I think because I'm in 100% complete remission, the chances of my tumor not coming back improve.*

He then talked about the different types of transplants. Allosomething (allogeneic) which would be a related match. Matt and Dad are going to be tested. Matt has the highest chance at 25%. Dad has a 1% chance. Auto-something (autologous) is where they would take my stem cells, knock me on my butt with chemo, and give them back to me. The last option is Allo-something (allogeneic) which would use stem cells from someone not related to me. They would do a national search and find a match through the registry of people on the donor list. The problem with that is the Graft versus Host Disease stuff. This is where the cells of the donor and my cells fight each other. A lot of shit can come from this and it can be fatal. Holy Cow… it was a lot of information. What I did hear was the chances go up to 80% cure rate after a transplant.

Here's what I think: I don't want to deal with this shit again. I want to do all I can do now and whatever happens, happens. If going through this crap a little longer means never dealing with this again, I can do that. What I want someone to say is, "You are going to have to do this, and then you are going to have to do that." I get a little tired of waiting to find out the next course of treatment. But right now I have to focus on my next round of chemo and then we can go from there. The One Day at a Time thing sometimes slips away, and I don't like it when that happens. I'll write more on this whole transplant thing later.

Today was a good day. I just got back from hanging out with Mary Ann at some bar. I met Brian E. (an AHS grad a year ahead of me) who had a sarcoma in his shoulder. He is in remission. It was so nice to talk to someone who has gone through it and knows what the hell is going on. He had heavy doses of chemo like me and knows what it feels like to be completely exhausted. I enjoyed the evening and so did he. He seemed ready to help somebody and give back. OK, my eyes are burning. I'm out.

I'm cancer free today and every day for the rest of my life.

BLAKE and I met because of Kim (my teammate at UT who took me under her wing). He worked at The University of California Irvine where Kim served as an assistant basketball coach. In October of 2001, Blake came to Austin and we went to the Texas-Colorado football game. Blake was so taken with the "Hook 'em, Horns" hand sign that he made up a hand sign to go with the UC Irvine Anteaters. (It doesn't hold a candle to our sign!) I had only known Blake for about six months when I got sick. We acted like we had known each other for years. He wrote me letters, encouraging emails, and sent me funny pictures. Whenever he was in the Dallas area, he would visit. He would call, make me laugh, and make me forget I was sick. Blake would do anything for me.

MORGEN and I played summer basketball together and against each other in college. She earned a scholarship to Kansas State. Morgen was in nursing school in Arlington when I got sick. Having her here in town was a gift. When I think of Morgen, I think of sunflowers. Like them, Morgen is beautiful, blond and happy. Being around Morgen always made me feel better. She would come over just to watch TV, just to talk, or just to be a friend. Morgen would do anything for me.

Meg & Morgen May, 2002

ALLY is a cancer survivor (Hodgkins lymphoma). Her mom is a cancer survivor (non-Hodgkins lymphoma). Ally was a volleyball player at the University of Wisconsin who got sick after her senior year. I met Ally because Meggan had transferred from Texas to Wisconsin. While I was in the hospital, Meggan called to tell me about Ally and how she thought we could relate because of our similar stories. She was right. It was great talking to someone who knew the unknowns, knew the anxieties and understood the emotions. Even though Ally lived back home in California, she always offered just the right help. She did so much just by calling, being there, listening, and sharing. Ally would do anything for me.

Chapter 14 July 2002

July 1:
Oh my goodness, it's July. I can't say much about the weather because I didn't get out until about 8. It was so nice. Not hot. Not humid. And the sky was amazing. Pink, red, blue, gray. Simply beautiful. Let me catch us up:

I attended Katie's wedding this weekend and it was wonderful. Everything was so smooth, Katie and Frank seemed so happy, and it just felt good. Katie looked gorgeous. I was pretty quiet this weekend and I don't think it was because I was tired. I think I was just looking at all of the other girls with their tans, their muscles, their hair, and wanting that again. The no hair thing really doesn't bother me that much. I just want to run again. I want the muscles. I want to go outside in the sun and not burn to a crisp. I was also thinking about marriage and how FAR OFF down the road that is. I know it has a lot to do with my current situation. I have so many things I want to do and marriage is one of them, but right now it doesn't even register.

Sunday, Cousin Molly came over and she treated me to a movie. I think I've had more things paid for during this time than in my five years of college. There have to be some perks, right? We saw Bourne Identity. I could look at Matt Damon all day. He is just a beautiful person and that smile—no words.

Today, I shaved. Shaved all of my dead hair south of the border. It's so bare THERE. No marks. Nothing. It's kinda nice. Maybe guys like the no hair thing EVERYWHERE— probably not.

I just realized something these last few days. If I have to do the transplant, that chemo must be some strong shit. I realized that the chemo for the transplant must kill off my bone marrow. Damn. I'm taking strong chemo now and it's not killing my bone marrow. Oh, vomit.

Moving on...Mom told me yesterday not to worry about whether or not Matt is a match. I don't think I am. I just want him to be one. I obviously know things are not in my control and this transplant proves that even more. If Matt is a match, then I would think I would use his. If he's not, then use mine—if we even have to do one. I keep saying "if I have to do one," but I really don't believe that any more. Anyway, I think everything will just keep moving on down the line. If this happens, then this, then that, and on and on. OK, time for bed.

I'm cancer free today and every day for the rest of my life.

July 5:

It's been a couple of days, so let me try to catch up before I fall asleep. I had a great 4th of July. I spent it with Sarah in Dallas. We watched the fireworks from her parking garage. It was a great show.

Yesterday, 3 people were killed in the LAX airport. They have not ruled out terrorism. I don't understand and I never will. I really have a lot to say, but I think I waited a little late. Kind of tired.

I'm invited to 3 weddings tomorrow—Kelli Tull (AAU teammate), Dianna Reynolds (one of my AAU coaches), and Cousin Mark (Molly's brother). Mark is getting married in Houston. Mom and I are going to Kelli's because it's closer. Dad and Matt are going to Mark's.

I'm cancer free today and every day for the rest of my life.

July 6:

OK, I'm back and feeling refreshed. On July 2, I asked Dr. Deur about the bone marrow transplant. He basically told me I'll be doing it. He said the size of the tumor is what scared him. He said the chemo will be "industrial strength." Great. No problem—just what I was hoping for. I really would like to talk to somebody who has done this—just to get a "heads up." I don't know for sure what it all entails. The doctors really haven't told me exact details. Matt will be tested Monday, and we'll find out in a week if he is a match. That would be awesome. I have a pretty good feeling about it.

OK, I was going to go on and on being philosophical, but I need to get ready for another wedding.

I'm cancer free today and every day for the rest of my life.

July 8:

Round 7. It's kinda sad, but I was excited to see my nurse friends. Yeah, that's pathetic. This is almost over. It's crazy how the mood changes with repetition. I think I was pretty nervous the first time at Arlington Memorial for Round 2. But now, I'm just ready to go and get it done. I have been looking forward to these last two rounds since March.

I hope when I'm done with all this, I still have the ONE DAY AT A TIME attitude. I've been making "plans"—like going down to Austin or seeing Meggan K. in Chicago before the transplant. I think I'm doing that to give me something to look forward to. When I'm done with this, I want to live like I don't have a tomorrow.

It's going to be great walking out of here after Round 8…knowing I won. Anywho, let me cover the topics, Matt's Date, Bone Marrow, Goals, Blah:

MATT'S DATE: Some girl he met on the internet. She's from Seattle or something. She's an athlete (finally), an

English teacher, and her name is Megan S. They had a date last night and he said they went to some bar and she went out without make-up. Points for her.

I just hope Matt doesn't move too fast. It sounds like she wanted to meet somebody and we all know Matt needed to meet someone. I'll be watching her. This time the grading scale gets a little tougher. Like Mom said, he is trying so hard. He just wants to do good. I love him so much. He got tested for the bone marrow transplant today. We'll find out in a week or so. Oh, that would be so nice.

BONE MARROW TRANSPLANT: Yeah, really don't want to talk about it. I've heard it's rough...I'm sure it is, but we'll deal with that later.

GOALS: Really don't know why the hell I wrote that. How about RANDOM THINGS OF WHAT I WOULD LIKE TO DO. Yeah, I like this topic.

—Run in the Danskin next June.
—Visit Meggan K. in Chicago, her sister Katie in Wisconsin, Erin at the University of Connecticut, Brenda who has moved to Colorado, Blake and Kim in California. Oh, what fun.

What I do think about is what do I do when I'm done?

What are you supposed to do? Do I go straight to work? Do I still live in the area? If I do the transplant, I'll be 24 when I'm ready to go. Is that too old to travel and see people? Hell, I don't know. So many good times ahead.

Alrighty, got a bag of cytoxan flowin'. Feeling good. Got my steroids and I'll be feeling a lot better in a little bit. Peace out.

I'm cancer free today and every day for the rest of my life.

Meg with UT teammate, California Kim

July 9:

I got a stomach cramp in the morning and I had just had a spinal tap…so when I moved, my head pounded.

I had some visitors yesterday and that was nice. Brenda, Lily (AAU teammate), Taryn (Texas teammate), Mary Ann, and Gramps. Zac came by and we talked about his transplant. He said it depends on what your definition of bad is, but he didn't think it was that bad. He lost 30 pounds. He is in remission. It was great talking to him. I enjoy talking to people who have gone through this. It's nice to relate and kind of make fun of the whole situation.

I think Kim and her mom might come by today as well as Virginia, another Texas teammate. I love visitors. They make the time go by faster. This is day 3 and things are going well. Except for yesterday's drowsiness, this round has been pretty good. Appetite isn't the best, but that's OK.

I'm cancer free today and every day for the rest of my life.

July 10:

Today is a good one. I've got my steroids and I'm good to go. Kim came by and we had a great visit. Carmen (Texas softball player) and one of her friends came by, too. It was cool. I think some others might come by later. Visitors help so much. It's so uplifting and energizing. I'm out.

I'm cancer free today and every day for the rest of my life.

July 13:

Oh, hello. I'm done with that hospital trip. Thursday and Friday are a blur. It's amazing. I have no idea what happened. Chemo is supposed to be your friend and all because it's killing the cancer, but I really don't like it. I feel so large right now. Dr. P. (on call for Dr. Deur) called Adriamycin the "Red Devil." You got that right. Damn, that stuff sucks. I really don't recall much over the last few days. The phone rang, but I sure couldn't tell you who called. Lara came by last night and it was so great seeing her. She always lifts me up. A few times today I just wanted to cry. It's hard to keep getting back up. I know I have to but, damn, it's hard.

I'm watching the WNBA right now. Yeah, nothing else is on. Not a big fan. I just like watching the players I played against.

Matt just got here. He is taking that internet girl and her mom out to Billy Bob's tonight. I think they spent the night at the country house last night. Poor guy. He is trying so hard. I just don't want him to get hurt. Now, I know he is just wanting to get to know the girl, but geeze—easy buddy. I don't know. He's 25 and he can do whatever he wants. I have just noticed some of the patterns and I don't want this to be "another one."

Yes, I'm tired and very bloated. Peace out.

I'm cancer free today and every day for the rest of my life.

July 15:

*Helloooooo…I must say I **love** living. So many times I go to bed smiling because I know of all the good things coming my way. Yesterday was a good day, too. We all just hung around the house. I did absolutely nothing. Timeout: I took 2 too many Senakot laxatives yesterday—YIKES!!*

Oh, the preliminary results show Matt is probably not a match. It looks like I'll be doing the auto-something transplant. Fine by me. That means a longer break. I can go visit some people. It also means quicker recovery and no Graft vs Host Disease. But it does mean lower percentages of a long term cure. Seriously, who cares about percentages. You're either alive or you're not. There's not a big difference between 60% and 80%. I'm going to do all I can and then LIVE. Amen.

It's at the point in the treatment where I have an agenda and can start checking stuff off. One more round of chemo— CHECK. I'll have my scans and biopsy to make sure I'm in remission, have my little break, do the transplant, and MOVE ON.

It's great to live one day at a time, but it's so nice to think about plans. Yes. I love thinking about California, my new muscular body, visiting friends, meeting new people, going out.

I'm cancer free today and every day for the rest of my life.

July 16:

Spinal Tap #14. Chemo…blah, blah. Holy Cow, my face itches. &^%$. Steroids, you are not my friend.

July 18:

I had two awesome days. Yesterday, Eryn came up around Happy Hour time. Eryn, Megan C., Mary Ann, and

I headed to Fort Worth for some drinks and to hear Zac's band—which we didn't. We got the date wrong. Oops. It was great just hanging out and talking.

Today, Mom and I surprised Matt and Gram at the golf course. Fun times. After lunch, Matt and I went out to the chipping green. Not too bad if I do say so myself. Little hot with the turban, though.

Then, I checked out Mitra's new place. So cute. She's going to do so well in medical school. I'm happy for her. I'm also pumped she is so close to Arlington. Tonight for dinner, it was me, Mitra, Matt, and Megan S.—the new girl. She was great. Smart. Funny. Cute and just cool. It was just a real pleasant time. Oh, it was a great day. I took a Xanax so I should be checking out pretty soon. Good Night.

I'm cancer free today and every day for the rest of my life.

Brian's visit

July 19:

Oh, what another great day! My hemoglobin is a little low, so I'll get a transfusion early in the morning before Jill S.'s wedding. (Jill and her twin Amy played against me in AAU and later when they were at Texas Christian University.) I felt so weird today. Every time I stood up, my legs felt so weak and I felt like I was going to pass out. Little scary sometimes. Later this afternoon, Brian M. came over. We had a great time just chillin'. He is such a good guy and seems to have it together and has some good things going for him. He talked about wanting to see the Dave Matthews Band at Red Rocks in Colorado! I'll go. For sure.

Mom and I went to get some Mexican food tonight. Not the best. Little gasy right now. Then, we got a treat from Emily Hunter and her mom. Emily just had her arm removed last week to get rid of the rest of the cancer. She looked great. She was smiling and so happy to be alive. Dang, life is so precious. How amazing for this 16-year-old girl to be smiling from ear to ear, looking beautiful after having her arm amputated! I was actually happy for Emily. I don't know if I could have said that if I had not had cancer myself. Cancer puts you in a different spot. You don't have many options. It's not like you can try this, and see what happens. Try that and see what happens. Your only choices are life or death. You do this to stay alive. You do that, so you don't die. Cancer gives you perspective. I was happy for Emily because she was alive.

Oh, just one more round of chemo. This is almost over and will soon be just a memory. Dang! That's so much fun to think about.

Even though I'm getting a four hour nap tomorrow, I'm off to bed.

I'm cancer free today and every day for the rest of my life. Amen.

July 22:

Whoa, Nellie! A few rough days I must say. The handwriting might suck because the arm sucks. More on that in a moment. These past few days have felt like weeks.

Saturday, I went to Jill S.'s wedding. Simple. Pretty. Happy. It was nice. I had a transfusion that morning, so things started early. At the wedding, I saw a few girls I used to play ball against. It's weird to think that 5 or 6 years ago we were playing against each and now so many of them are getting married.

Here has been the drama over the last few days. Saturday, I either had bone pain from the neupegen shots or from steroid withdrawals. Either way, it sucked. I spent the night with Gram and Gramps and my legs were so restless. It wasn't as bad as THAT night a while ago, but it wasn't pleasant. I took a warm bath at about 8 a.m. and it helped a little. Then, my friggin' arm started hurting. What in the hell? That pain was in the bone, but it felt like it was going all the way to the nerves. It hurt. Right now, it's weak because it's been twitching for 2 days. It kinda reacts like a seizure. Yeah, the past two days have just not been fun. It's just been reminding us we are still a part of the cancer fight. We want it to be over. That won't come too soon, but it just wears on you. Damn.

*I also hate when something hurts because you think, "What the hell is wrong?" For real, "Do I have a brain tumor? Do I have Parkinson's?" That's really not calming to think about. But my arms have really been bothering me. Is it the withdrawals from prednisone? Is it seven rounds of chemo and my body is saying **BACK OFF BITCH**. My body has had so much crap put into it. Steroids, chemo, Celebrex, Keflex, Lortab, Tylenol, Benadryl, antibiotic after antibotic, birth control for all my wild and crazy sex—the list goes on.*

It's just a lot of crap. My arms are tired and I'm ready to be pain free.

I found out about an hour ago I will get the whole month of September off. That means vacation time. I'm quite pumped about it.

I'm cancer free today and every day for the rest of my life.

July 24:

Tomorrow I'm headed to Austin. I'm having a little get-together with my friends because I basically want to tell them "Thank You." I'm thinking about doing it in a prayer.

Dear Heavenly Father,

Thank you for this day and thank you for this gathering. I wanted to get these people together to say thank you. These people along with so many others have been there for me since day one. My remission and my recovery would not have been possible without these people. They have given me strength, laughter, and support. The chemo has helped, but I know these people have saved my life. It does sound odd to say I have been blessed as I sit here with no hair, but I truly have been blessed with wonderful people and these people will always be in my heart. Thank you for everything.
Amen.

Yeah, probably won't make it through that one.

Anywho—I'm fat. My belly is so large. Is this the water retention or the dozen cookies? I know I'm supposed to pack it in before the transplant, but I think I've gone a little overboard. Geeze. And, I really don't know why I care. Maybe because I think my body is so disgusting anyway, and I don't want it to get worse. I'll probably be in the 1% who gain 30 pounds during the transplant.

I met some new people at Dr. Deur's office today and honestly thought, "Oh, I wish I had met these people earlier.

I won't get to see them that much." Seriously, what is my problem? Yeah, you won't see them much because you'll be done with this shit soon. Moron.

Sometimes my thoughts really worry me. Por ejemplo, this cancer thing is serious and I don't think I realize that 90% of the time. Maybe that's good. But just the fact I was a little sad and wasn't going to get my blood drawn and see the nurses is a little troubling.

Back to my fatness. I'm staring at my legs right now— Hey, Pigs in a Blanket. They are just so nasty. Not a speck of muscle. Not a glimpse…not a hope…nothing…Oh, well. I'm not tired. That's really unfortunate since I'm getting up in 6 hours. I'll just go take a pill. I'm out.

I'm cancer free today and every day for the rest of my life.

July 28:

What a wonderful weekend! On Thursday night, I invited a few people over to Lara's apartment for a little ice cream and cake action. We had a great time and I barely made it through the prayer.

Friday night, I went to eat at Pappasitos with Lara and Tracy. Fatty Patties. It was great. Oooh, I had a little breakdown in the car. I just kept thinking about people going out, having fun, going to concerts, and planning things. It just made me a little sad thinking about all of the things I'm missing out on. Even though I wouldn't be in Austin, I'd be doing something. I sure as hell wouldn't be hanging out in hospitals, meeting nurses, and learning about blood counts. I know I have said this 100 times, but I'm tired of it. The newness has worn off. Blah, blah, blah…

Good News—I walked two miles Saturday. I RAN a lap. It was awesome. My goal is to be able to run a mile before the transplant. Oh, I would love it. It would be even better if I came back a Lance Armstrong. No lactic acid and a leaner body. Right, right…

Back to reality. Lance won the Tour de France. Incredible. I really can't say anything that describes that accomplishment. But I know he has given so many people hope and a chance to fight.

I'm done here. Oh, before I forget. Yeah, got called a "sir" this week. It went like this: Hello SIR. How can I help you? I thought this: "You can lean forward, so I can punch you in the face." Not my proudest moment.

I'm cancer free today and every day for the rest of my life.

July 29:

Going to be honest here. Today I felt like complete shit. I had the PMS funk. I hate that crap. I'm real excited about starting my period at the hospital. That really grosses me out to think I'll be nauseated, have purple ankles while having to change my friggin' tampon. Not my idea of a good time. I go in for Round 8 tomorrow. I'm not as fired up about it as I originally thought. I think Aunt Flo has something to say about that. Really don't like her much. Last check-in, last drive for treatment, last dose of metha—whatever the hell that evil drug is called. That's exciting. I wonder if those lovely fevers will pop up on me. Probably jinxed myself. Crap. I walked 2¼ miles today at a pretty good pace. I was proud of myself. I talked to Matt tonight. He hasn't felt too good the last few days. Throwing up and crap like that. Weak fever though—only 102°. HA!

I'm cancer free today and every day for the rest of my life.

ZAC was a high school classmate. I heard he had cancer when I was a junior in college. He was diagnosed with multiple myeloma. Zac was the cutie in the high school's drum line. He had this James Dean look going for him. He and I were in student council together. He won sophomore and junior prince for our Homecoming celebration. I was nominated with him my junior year. I lost.

Zac was the first person I knew my age who had cancer. My first reaction was, "Awwwww, that's horrible." I had no idea. Today, my heart hurts and I almost throw up when I hear the news of anyone's cancer diagnosis.

I'm sure Zac hurt when he heard about me. He called several times. He came to visit me in the hospital and always offered advice and encouragement. It always helped me to talk to him about it.

Zac relapsed a couple of years after his first bone marrow transplant with his brother as a donor. He has undergone a second transplant with another sibling (Zac has six brothers and sisters) donating stem cells.

Even though Zac wasn't in my circle of close friends, we are both in The Tough Club. That's a forever bond.

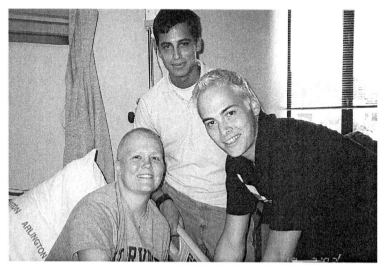

Zac (foreground) and his brother Adam who was
Zac's marrow donor, with Meg

I first met **BRIAN M**. while he was dating my roommate Eryn. He was a friend of California Kim's. Brian is one of those guys who will support you, laugh with you, shoot the &^%$ with you, and will never leave you. When I first got sick, Brian drove up from his job in Houston to join the group on watch in the ICU. Even after he changed jobs and moved to New Mexico, Brian always stopped by my house when he was "passing through" even though my house was always out of the way. When I called Brian, he always made the time even if he didn't have any. Plain and simple, Brian is a good guy. Brian would do anything for me.

July 30:
While I'm waiting for Round 8—the last round—to start, I think I'll write a letter to Lara.

Dear Lara,
This is one of those letters you need to save. So when you are having a bad day, you can read this and feel better. When we are 50-something years old, chatting about life, and if I have lost perspective on things or become "not me," I order you to read this to me. OK? Great.

It's Tuesday afternoon. 3 p.m. Round 8 is almost underway. They've got a bag of fluids getting me hydrated. I'm so excited about feeling like complete shit in 3 days.

This part of the letter is what you'll remind me of if I ever sway from these ideas or philosophies. OK?

—I don't have control. Bad things are going to happen. Have enough faith that things will be all good.
—Live one day at a time.
—Do not be someone who hates her job.
—Never be afraid to try new things.
—Dance like no one is watching.
—Live life like I have a terminal illness. Girl, this shit is almost over. Let me just share a few things I'm looking forward to:
—Running (For Real)
—Being Sore (this means I have muscle)
—Driving myself to Austin
—Not worrying if people have washed their hands
—Using hair things
—Visiting Friends

—*Not knowing the TV schedule*

—*Not having a personal relationship with the cast of the"RealWorld"*

—*Thinking about sex without vomiting*

—*Having a cord-free boob*

—*Growing hair EVERYWHERE—down there, too*

—*Not taking 6 pills a day*

—*Not peeing red and green*

—*Dancing with you and all my friends*

—*Not worrying that "Can I help you, sir" might be directed toward me*

—*Going on vacation and drinking Long Islands*

—*Not knowing the hospital custodians' family history*

—*Having my own place*

—*Driving after sunset*

—*Competing in a triathlon*

—*Running a marathon*

—*Hiking through the mountains of Colorado*

—*Snow skiing*

—*Calling my friends and saying call me back at this number and not leaving a hospital room number*

—*Not hearing I should try Ensure*

—*Getting my dimples back*

—*Not tripping over my groshong*

—*Reading books that don't talk about cancer*

—*Shot free days*

—*Transfusion free days*

—*Doctor appointment free days*

—*No worries about my health*

—*Putting the aforementioned priorities into effect*

Whew! That was fun. Now, save this letter so at Christmas and Thanksgiving when our families get together, we can break this out.

Thank you, Lara, for everything. I cherish you greatly. I could write 10 more pages on how much you mean to me, but this Metha—kiss my ass stuff—is kicking in.

Big Hugs and a lot of love. May God Bless you every day.

> *I love you so much,*
> *Meg Brown*

Chapter 16 August 2002

August 1:

Man, the summer just flies by when you are out basking in the sun every day, exercising with a vengeance, not watching hours of TV, and making multiple trips to the clinic and hospital every week. Anywho…It's day 3 of Round 8 and I feel great. No side effects. I had a little headache, but that has been it. I really hope I'm not jinxing myself, but I'm cruising. I think since I have been so excited about being done, maybe that has carried over.

I have thought a little bit about the future. First of all, I think I have a say in when I'll have the bone marrow transplant. So, I'm hoping Lara and I can go up to Connecticut and see Erin the first weekend in October. It would be even better if I could go to the Texas/OU game. That might be pushing it, but that would be cool. Here's my plan:
—Continue to feel great
—Start exercising more
—Lift weights, yoga, and dance exercise class
—Visit Meggan in Chicago
—Run a mile by the end of September
Well, that's the plan at least.

I'm cancer free today and every day for the rest of my life.

August 2:

Oh my, I'm still feeling good. I had a tiny fever this morning, and, actually, right now I have a big friggin' headache. Damn. Besides the fever, I had a great day today. I saw Lara's Mom, Charlie from church, and talked to Lara, Brian, Aunt Beth, Sandy (Kim's mom), and a few more. I finished my last bag of chemo this morning at 10:30. It felt great. I have one more bag of leucovorin, (a drug which helps my body recover from the gallons of chemo drugs), a spinal tap on Tuesday, and then **I AM DONE.** YESSSS! It feels so good to be done.

Emily Hunter's scans came back today **ALL CLEAR.** Life is good. She still has to do a few more rounds and then, she'll be done. I'm so happy for her.

I'm cancer free today and every day for the rest of my life.

August 3:

I finished Round 8 today. It feels good to know I won't be going back to the hospital in three weeks for chemo.

I'm cancer free today and every day for the rest of my life.

August 4:

Today was great. I did some exercises and tonight I visited with Emily. She was not as energized tonight as she was immediately after her surgery. She has to go back in for chemo tomorrow. She will do two to four more rounds. What the hell? I know she is thinking, "Does it ever end?" She will be in my prayers.

The highlight of the day was a visit by Lara. She stayed for about 3 hours. I love it when she comes to visit. It brightens my day. Love her.

Anywho, I'm so pumped about having two months of freedom. I must remember I'm not going to have tons of energy for about 2 more weeks. Then, it's Let Your Hair Down and time to have some fun.

Going back into the hospital for the transplant is really going to suck. Fo sho. But I can't worry about that. Time to think about today and having fun today.

Mom and Gram go get their mammograms tomorrow.

It was a year ago at this time that Mom and I were in Idaho with the Kohnens and the Oeths (Meggan's parents and future in-laws) hiking, running, swimming in waterfalls, soaking up the sun, eating our weight in milkshakes and malts, laughing, and, of course, having an absolute blast. It's definitely been a long year. One we'll always remember and thank God for healing us. Thank you, Heavenly Father.

I'm cancer free today and every day for the rest of my life.

August 5:

I just wanted to share that I'm friggin' bald again. What the hell? My hair was growing back good. I even had a hair line. Yeah, I'm totally bald, as in slick, in some places—like the back of my head and on the right side—nothing. DOH! Really hope it grows back some before the transplant so I can get an idea of what it might look like. My other thing this morning is I'm really going to miss the nurses on Station 32. They were so sweet. Of course, any one would miss a place where they are well-liked, but they really helped me through the days.

That is it for now.

I'm cancer free today and every day for the rest of my life.

August 6:

YESSSSSS. 16th spinal tap today. Round 8 is completely finished and I just threw up. Neat. Mom and Gram got their mammograms back today and they are good to go. Praise the Lord. Amen. Wee bit tired, so I'm going to hit the bed.

I'm cancer free today and every day for the rest of my life.

August 7:

Yeah, yesterday after the spinal tap I just felt gross and out of my element. The nurses at Dr. Deur's gave me a card *and a present for being done. Too sweet. My vent for the day has to do with me. Shocker. I'm tired of looking like this. I don't feel like a girl. I have lost my femininity. It doesn't help that I kinda dressed like a dude before this, but at least I could get away with it because of my hair. Now, I wear the same clothes, walk the same way (which doesn't help my case), throw on a bandana, and I'm a pretty cute guy. This is what I feel goes through the brains of the general public. "Oh, he has on hoop earrings and he has painted his toenails. He just signed his name Meg. Let's look at his driver's license. Oh, Mary Margaret. She has hair in this picture. Oh, he's a girl. OH MY." Even if they aren't thinking that, I look like a damn pirate with my hoop earrings and bandana. It's quite annoying and I would like it to stop.*

Done with the venting—for now. Other news—I have no idea.

I'm cancer free today and every day for the rest of my life.

August 7:

Got some not so fun news this morning which has led me to my second entry of the day. I'm going to have to do more chemo, dammit. This two months off thing was a pile of shit. They need to give me more chemo before they collect my stem cells. I thought 8 rounds would finish it off. And now I'm looking at Round 9. It's all bullshit. That's really all I have to say about that.

I'm cancer free today and every day for the rest of my life.

August 8:

The day got better yesterday. I guess there was really only one way to go. Last night, Mary Ann and I drove to Dallas to hang out with Megan C. It's always a good time when you talk about sex. That got me thinking. When the hell am I going to have sex? I had my three year theory, but that was in October. Already lost a year on that one. Damn Cancer. Another side effect—sex will be delayed. Sonofa.

Here's my new theory: I probably won't be having sex during the transplant while I'm in the bubble. Just a gut feeling. I would like to be in love with the guy. High Standards I know. But looking at my past boyfriend record, I haven't had too many "in love" experiences. What I'm getting at is I'm not going to be having sex for while. And once you get to be 23 or 24, I really don't want to "get it over with." That's just dumb. Well, I was just thinking about it today since the thought of kissing doesn't make my stomach turn.

Moving on…Everything was good today. I walked 1½ miles. I **WILL** be running by the end of September. Indeed. OK, I'm getting tired. Tomorrow night, Mary Ann is throwing a dessert party for me. Definitely not losing the love handles.

I'm cancer free today and every day for the rest of my life.

August 12:
Count update: Hemoglobin = 7 (red blood cells which carry oxygen to the body), Platelets = 2,000, (blood cells which form clots), NE# = 0 (neutrophylls are baby white cells). Not your best. No wonder I have been so friggin' tired. I don't know if my legs are sore due to lack of activity or lack of blood to the muscles. I really don't know anything. I'm out.

I'm cancer free today and every day for the rest of my life.

August 13:
Chalk this day up to boring as hell and tired. Transfusion from 9 a.m. to 2 p.m. Watched TV. Boring, boring, boring.

I'm cancer free today and every day for the rest of my life.

August 15:

Yesterday was Gram's 81st birthday. I was officially depressed yesterday morning. It was awful. This is short because I want to get back to my book and I'm tired. I walked 2 miles today. I'm tired. Good night.

I'm cancer free today and every day for the rest of my life.

Meg, Mitra, Cathy at Mitra's White Coat Ceremony

August 20:

It's been a good few days. I had a great time at Mitra's White Coat Ceremony, her initiation into med school. She looked great and seemed excited and happy to be doing it. Monday, Mom and I left for Dallas. I have a few days of testing to do. Yesterday, I had my scans and tomorrow will be the bone marrow biopsy. For the scans, I had to drink two huge cups of Barium. Holy Cow, that stuff tastes like ass. You would think they could give nauseated patients something besides friggin' Barium for their tests. I'm tired. Peace out.

I'm cancer free today and every day for the rest of my life.

August 24:

Does this cancer thing ever level out? It doesn't seem like it. Friday, Mom, Dad, and I go to see Dr. Berryman so he can tell me when I'm going to get started on this transplant thing. A few days before, he told me I might not have two months off and could do the transplant as early as next week. WHAT? What happened to the big "break?" After a few tears, I accepted that and figured it would be best. I would be done and healthy by the holidays. Great…I can do all of my vacationing over the holidays. We are all feeling pretty good about things because we are ready to get the transplant over and done with. Bye, Bye, Cancer, Forever. No more shots. Hello, hair. You get the picture. OK, Dr. Berryman starts off by saying, "I have some disturbing news." Shit. Shit. Shit. You never want a doctor to start a sentence that way. They sent my bone marrow off to UT Southwestern labs and the results showed 0.3% abnormal T-Cells—whatever the hell that means. Basically, it means there might still be some cancer in the bone marrow. Kaka. But the machine could have jacked up. Because my marrow is so weak anyway, damaged cells might have looked cancerous. My opinion: How in the hell could the chemo have gotten everything but 0.3? That's a bunch of bullshit if you ask me. They don't think the cancer is coming back, but if the machines didn't pick up the cancer during round 6, how could 0.3 survive three more rounds of chemo? Dr. Berryman said false positives do happen and the machine could have had an error. That's good. In summary, I'll for sure be doing a transplant. We just don't know which one. Shit. The worst part of this whole cancer thing is all the damn curve balls. There are no plans. As soon as you make them, it seems like cancer interferes. So now, I'll be chillin' for a few more days until another bone marrow biopsy on September 3. (Big Sigh.) Basically, we still don't *know what the hell is going on. Mom is right, though. I will pray that the machines are **right**. How bad would it be if I did the WRONG transplant? Vomit. But I **don't** have cancer.*

*I'm cancer free **TODAY** and EVERY DAY FOR THE REST OF MY LIFE!!!*

August 25:

I talked to Angie tonight. She's one of Dr. Deur's nurses. Sweet girl. She called to check and see how I was doing after the consult. That was so nice of her to call. She didn't know if she was crossing any boundaries by calling. Nope. Not on my end. I'll take all the friends I can get. She's a cool girl. Tomorrow…what will I do? Good question. I'll figure something out. Good Nite.

I'm cancer free today and every day for the rest of my life.

Chapter 17

September 2
– September 27, 2002

September 2:

It's been a while so I'll catch us up. I went down to Austin on Wednesday. Tracy met me in Waco again. She is so sweet. I hope my friends don't get tired of coming after me. I know it's to pick up a friend, but 3 hours out of the day is a lot. Then, to take my ass back…I get annoyed with it, so who knows what they are feeling?

Thursday, I saw Kathleen (UT swimmer and member of my teaching cohort) at her school and got to see some other people. The downer of the trip was finding out that Christie, a girl in my kinesiology classes who came to visit me at the hospital, might have cancer. They found a mass on her CT scan and her blood work was not good. She has lost some weight and not on purpose. I talked to her and I really didn't know what to say. I haven't heard from her, so I'm assuming the diagnosis is not good. I'm hoping my assumptions are wrong. It's not fair. I hate that I know what she is about to go through. It sucks and it's bullshit.

Today, I'm a little tired of the weekend's festivities. Mary Ann took me to see The Lion King last night. It was amazing. I absolutely loved it. I would be so broke, but I would love to go to New York and just watch Broadway shows. Oh, how fun.

Tomorrow is the bone marrow biopsy. Not too worried about that. It'll be clear. I'm off to read and call some people.

I'm cancer free today and every day for the rest of my life. Amen.

September 3:

Good day today. I walked a few miles this morning and walked pretty fast, too. Good workout. Then, Mom and I headed over to Baylor for another bone marrow aspirate. OUCH! I'm going to say this one was a little more painful than the others. It's all good because it's going to come back negative, and then I can move on with the transplant.

I met a guy about my age today, Art. He just got out of the hospital Friday from doing an auto transplant. He said he was weak for several days, but didn't have any nausea or any of the dreaded mouth sores. That's awesome. I hope I look as good as him 5 days after my AUTO transplant.

I find out my results Friday. I'm really not worried about it. I have to do a transplant. I would rather do my own, but you gotta do what makes you better.

Watched American Idol tonight. Kelly Clarkson is a goddess. She is so good. Big star for her. Fo sho.

Today Christie saw Dr. Kasper, the oncologist who treated me in Austin, for a bone marrow biopsy. She finds out everything Friday, but if it is a lymphoma, I hope it's something where the chemo isn't that bad and she doesn't have to do spinal taps. That is all for now.

I'm cancer free today and every day for the rest of my life.

September 6:

We are about to head to Dallas to find out what we are going to do. Today is a big day for all my cancer friends. Grady is having surgery, and Christie is getting the results of her biopsy. I haven't been feeling so hot lately. I have a little bit of a cold. I've been sleeping at least 10 hours a night with naps in between.

I'm cancer free today and every day for the rest of my life. I truly believe that.

OK, I'm back. Got good news today. The second bone marrow biopsy is still a measly 0.3%. That means the cancer has not grown. Dr. Berryman thinks the auto transplant will still work. They will collect my stem cells and send those off to check for cancer. If they are positive, then we will start looking for a donor. If we can't find a donor, then we will do the auto transplant and Dr. Berryman thinks the high doses of chemo and radiation will take care of things. What was good was talking about a cure forever. The shitty part is I will have Round 9 on Wednesday. He said I would get a high volume of chemo similar to that of a transplant. Matt said it good, "The big picture got better, but the details got shittier." Good call.

September 9:

Alrighty, I'll continue from yesterday. Still not feeling 100%. It's two days until September 11. Sometimes it feels like it all happened yesterday, it's still so hard to believe, and sometimes it seems like it happened years ago. TV stations have been doing anniversary type things all weekend and the city of New York has been having ceremonies of their own. I can't imagine what they are thinking and feeling. Do they wake up and cry every day? What do the kids say? How do you move on from something like that?

Oh, I hate thinking about that kind of stuff. So much sadness. What happened a year ago was bull and stuff like that should not happen. OK, I'm rambling…I've got to go to the bathroom. I'll write more later.

OK, I'm back. Tonight, my thoughts are so happy. Life can be so good. I hope I always realize that. I know this is a hard time for so many people and for our country. I can only hope they are surrounded by love and faith. For my own stuff, I know the days ahead might totally suck, but some days are so good, so simple, and so fun. Like tonight, Mary Ann, her boyfriend Whit, Brian E., his wife Autumn, and I went to dinner. It was wonderful. Oh, we laughed about stupid stuff and had such a good time. I loved it.

Today, I saw Grady in recovery. Feisty Fella. It was funny. He finds out big news on Wednesday. He's feeling everything is benign. I pray it will be. I also stopped by to see my 3rd grade teacher. She was one of the best. She has lung cancer. She was a little out of it. She said, "Meg, you cut your hair." Yeah, got crazy and shaved it. I heard she is expected to live a month. I didn't know what to say. I don't know if I'm numb to it or if I think she is going to be OK. Since I have talked to so many people who are doing well and who are survivors, I forget some people don't make it. Mrs. Breault was such a wonderful lady. So sweet. Always has been and always will be. May God be with her and her husband and comfort them. Oh, my eyes…time for bed.

Tomorrow is golf with Gram and dinner with Matt and Megan.

I'm cancer free today and every day for the rest of my life.

September 10:

In 20 minutes, it will be September 11. The day I check in for Round 9.

Dear Heavenly Father, tomorrow will be a hard day for so many people. Some people are still suffering physical and emotional pain. I hope that those who loved the innocent victims feel your love, find comfort in your love, and are able to love again. Please let tomorrow be a day of remembrance and honoring of the lives lost. Bless our nation tomorrow and those who love it. Thank you and Love you. Amen.

What was I doing a year ago today? How many people remember? For some, this was the last day they saw their *husbands, wives, brothers, sisters, parents, friends. Every time I see it, I shake my head and say HOW? WHAT ARE THOSE PEOPLE GOING THROUGH AND THINKING? I have to remind myself sometimes that those people covered in soot are not actors, and it's ash from two of the largest buildings in the world. It's overwhelming to think about it. Tomorrow is going to be story after story. Are they going to re-live the day? I don't know how people heal, but I don't think reliving is the way to do it.*

OK, I'm going to stop and move on to a different topic: ME.

Tomorrow, I'm going in for a triple line thing. (These are the lines which will funnel all the chemo and support drugs into me.) We are leaving in about 5 hours. I'm going to look like ass. Who cares? It's weird, but I'm almost excited. I think because it's just another hurdle before it's all over. I hope. Or I'm just sick in the head and gross. OK. I'm fading out.

I'm cancer free today and every day for the rest of my life.

September 15:

So far things have been OK. I have only thrown up a few times. It seems like I'm bored and just ready to be done with all this shit. Dad said today, "I have a lot more of this stuff behind me than I do in front of me." So true. As of right now, my tummy is a little upset and my throat tastes like shit. I'll be getting some drugs here in a little bit and falling asleep quite soundly.

I'm cancer free today and every day for the rest of my life.

121

Meg taking a hospital walk in her bikini,
September 2002

September 17:

Today is going pretty good. Hell, it's only 8:45 in the morning. I think I got a little cocky yesterday with my food. I was eating whatever yesterday and today—not so much. Salty stuff sounds oh-so-good. I have slept well the past few nights. Thank you, Drugs. I think the plan is just to wait for my counts to drop and for me to feel like complete ass. Neat.

I talked to quite a few people yesterday. Dad and I went for a walk. It was nice to get out and about. I love watching people's reactions as I turn the corner with my IV pole and mask. It looks like they're worried I'm going to give them something. That's not how it works. I'm worried about them giving me something. It's great watching the kids. Hilarious. Here's this bald person, walking stiffly with a mask, and all you can see are my eyes. Hell, I'd be scared, too. The hardest part is finding things to do. Writing in my journal helps. I would like to write some poetry or do something productive.

It made me feel better when Brian E. said he didn't "accomplish" anything during his cancer "hiatus." He might have been lying, but he made me feel better. You see, at the beginning of this whole thing, I really thought I would have time to learn things and do more stuff since I'd have all of this free time on my hands. Not so much. I usually feel good for only 3 or 4 days before the next round of chemo. And I'm not going to learn new and interesting things 3 or 4 days before the next trip in. I could have a different mindset, but I don't. Holy Cow, my handwriting sucks!

Mrs. Breault died the other day. I really didn't feel anything. I don't know if I'm supposed to or what, but it really didn't affect me. She was pretty sick and I think they gave her about a month to live. She was out of it when I visited the other day. I really don't like saying this, but at least she is not suffering. How do you make sense of someone dying? It just sucks all the way around.

Anywho, I'm about to eat some yummy Cheerios and start my day.

I'm cancer free today and every day for the rest of my life.

September 19:
Did absolutely nothing today. My ass is getting flatter and flatter. I felt OK today, but I was so tired. I don't know if it was the medicine I took last night or if I was just exhausted. Yesterday, I had quite a few visitors and talked on the phone—real exciting I know—but it wore me out. Tyler (my favorite coach) and Mary (Mom's very good friend) came up today and that was fun.

I have had some time to think the last few days and it kinda weirds me out when I really start to think about life. Our family has been pretty "lucky" or blessed. I think of my situation and then I think of how much people hurt and ache when family members pass. Basically, so much can happen to people. Sickness, September 11, car accidents, freak accidents. How come some people live to be 105 while others get sick at age 2 with cancer? OK, like today, someone is caught on tape beating up her kid. What the hell? Two guys tonight jumped the 1st base coach in a major league baseball game. Why? What for? I don't understand.

I think sometimes it scares me. What's going to happen? Who likes it when bad things happen, but I think I worry something else might happen to our family or to our friends. And Holy Shit, what if Saddam blows up half the damn country. Then what? What happens when we die? Where do we go? What do we do? It's weird to think about life beyond cancer. It's sometimes hard to imagine it now, but I know one day I'm going to have hair, have a career, have muscles, and all that good stuff. I wonder if people really think about life. Will there be a year 3004 or whatever? Thinking about all of that stuff sends my brain spinning. I could go on about this forever, but I won't.

I'm cancer free today and will be every day for the rest of my life.

September 21:

Mom's Birthday. 57! Whoa! She looks awesome for an oldie. We had a great time yesterday. Her buddies Sheila and Pam came over to celebrate. So fun. Mom is so different from those ladies and I love it. They both spend more than 5 minutes on their make-up—which Mom doesn't. They have a lot more clothes (we are going to work on that for Mom) and they are such girls. Mom is so not a girl. I can't believe it took me so long to realize that. I just figured I got my tomboy status from Dad. Nope. Mom is a Tomboy. I love it.

OK, what the hell am I still doing here? It's day friggin'

11 in the damn hospital. Day friggin' 5, at least, of feeling fine. My counts are still at zero and it would be nice if they would recover (Ah-hem.) I'm forgetting that I don't live here. Really wish I hadn't adapted to this routine. Anywho, I've been watching Sportscenter for about 5 straight hours. I think it's time for bed.

Oh, my friggin' mouth is a little sore. It doesn't really hurt, but it feels like someone nailed me in the teeth. That would definitely suck to get those mouth sores. OK, clean mouth for me. It's clear. Smooth. Alrighty...

I'm cancer free today and every day for the rest of my life. Happy Birthday, Mom! I love you.

September 24:

Yes, I'm still here. Not kidding. I'm still in the hospital. **BUT** my counts are moving up. My bones are starting to hurt a little bit. I know this is a big surprise, but I didn't do much today. Dr. Berryman told me about my regimen for the transplant. I think he said 2 days of chemo and 3 days of radiation twice a day. The radiation will be total body. Fertility is a big question. I might already be infertile and Dr. Berryman said those chances are high. But my chances are better of getting my fertility back because I'm young. That makes me sad, but I would consider myself blessed if I'm married and wanting to have children. That means I'm in love and alive. Time for bed.

I'm cancer free today and will be every day for the rest of my life.

September 26:

Yesterday was Matt's 26th birthday.
Let me give you the update:
They are harvesting my stem cells for the

125

auto-transplant. I am currently lacking 1.5 million stem cells. DAMN! The minimum number of cells they want is 2 million. So here are the 3 possible scenarios:

1) *I collect enough stem cells Friday, they are clean, and I go home Saturday morning.*
2) *I don't collect enough Friday, but I do on Saturday. I go home.*
3) *I don't collect enough on both days and will have to do the allo transplant.*

I think the perfect picture would be this: I collect enough cells, the cells are clean, my bone marrow is sufficient, and I can do the auto-transplant. The not so best scenario would be this: I either can't get enough cells or they aren't clean. Either way, I would have to do the allo-transplant using an unrelated donor.

Dear Heavenly Father, I have not asked for a lot during this, but I want enough cells. I want them to be clean. I want to do the auto transplant. This has been enough of a challenge. I'll gladly pass on this. I am, however, grateful for there being perfect matches. Thank you for this day. Please watch after James (a leukemia patient I met during this round) and let his treatment be as short as possible. Amen.

Today Nurse Angela from Arlington Memorial came over to visit. She is so sweet. It was great visiting with her outside of HER hospital. Mary Ann and her college roommate Chelsea came over and we watched Friends. Oh, so funny. What else is going on? Lara is doing well. I kinda get jealous or envious when Lara talks about all the people she is hanging out with and how much fun she is having. I know I'll be back there one day, but it's just been so long. It would be so fun to be back in a familiar place with familiar people.

*Oh, things to think about for a few more months. Please I want to do the **Auto Transplant.***

Auto transplant for Meg Brown.

I wish my drug would kick in so I could write under the influence. Tomorrow is a big day. Please let it be a good one.

I'm cancer free today and every day for the rest of my life.

September 27:

Well, we got the news today. My stem cells are infected. So I am going to do the allo-transplant. SHIT! SHIT! SHIT!

Good news—I have two donors lined up from overseas. One, a 27-year-old woman, and the other, a 31-year-old man. This type of transplant would also mean a new immune system. Disturbing news—I'm still sick and I still have cancer. Also, this process could be more difficult because of the risk of Graft vs. Host Disease. So, I'm pretty tired thinking about this. Basically, I'm just disappointed. I still have cancer. I'm disappointed because for three months we were excited about doing the auto transplant. I'm disappointed because we thought I would just do radiation on the site (mediastinum). But that too has changed and now I'm going to have to do total body. It's a total roller coaster ride and I'm ready to get off. It is good the tests worked. If I had done the auto transplant, I would have relapsed a few months later and surviving would have been even more difficult. Vomit. But this is the next step and it's got to be done.

*One question: Dr. Berryman said the cells showed infection, but it was really small—like 0.1%. How did I do 9 rounds of chemo and still have 0.1? ONLY 0.1! **SHIT!** I think I'm over it. Maybe give me another day. I guess I won't end each entry with my "I'm cancer free today and every day for the rest of my life." Good Night.*

127

Chapter 18 — Survival Secrets: Doctors, Nurses, Technology

Oh, the medicine—yes—that would be the chemotherapy. It was hard to realize this stuff was helping me. As I was throwing up, and cussing the methotrexate, I had to remember the chemo was helping. It's the cancer I should hate.

My treatments were very aggressive and I had a lot of it. Because I was young, I could handle it. They sucked. I did realize the chemo was helping, but I still threw up. I still felt like crap, and it still sucked. But it saved my life. For that I am grateful.

Scientific advances played a part in my survival. Dr. Berryman sent my bone marrow for a special test after the ninth round. This was to make sure every trace of the 0.3% abnormal t-cells present before that round had been eradicated. That test showed the ninth round killed off some of those abnormal t-cells, but not all. I still had a measly 0.0%. This determined my course of transplant treatment. Without this test, believing I was in remission I would have done the auto transplant, relapsed a few months later, and died shortly after because my body would not have been able to handle any further chemotherapy. Just five years earlier, the standard testing wouldn't have picked up that tiny amount. We can all only hope researchers will continue to make strides and save more lives.

Words cannot describe the appreciation, admiration, and love I have for my doctors. My doctors were a patient's dream. If I had one hundred questions, they would take the time to answer each and every one. If I wanted to discuss my fears, my feelings, or the weather, they would listen and we would carry on a conversation like friends. They always made me feel like I was their only and most important patient.

Whenever I was about to go to the hospital or clinic, my dad would always say, "Hey, you get to go see your friends." And that's exactly what my nurses were to me. They were my friends. They loved me and I loved seeing them. They always made me feel like they had been thinking about me for days or weeks or however long it had been since the last time we had seen each other. I knew they hadn't, but they made me feel that way.

I had more great nurses than I can tell you about. But here are examples of four terrific ones.

ANGIE was my mom's nurse at Dr. Deur's infusion clinic. Hands down, the sweetest person I have ever met. I loved it when she was my nurse—probably because she always laughed at my jokes. Angie would call, come over to visit, ask my mom about me, send me cards, and was always so sincerely interested in me. She is honest, compassionate, supportive, and loving.

ANGELA was my nurse for the first round in Arlington (which was round #2). At first, I liked her because she was young and I thought she was cute. I thought, "Hey, Matt should like this girl." She enjoyed seeing me just as much as I enjoyed seeing her because it gave her a break from the old geezers on the rest of the oncology floor. Even when I went to a different hospital, she kept in contact. Angela is a good person with a loving soul.

JUDITH was another nurse in Arlington. Judith was there for me that day when I was surrounded by so much death in the hospital. She came into my room, hugged me, let me cry, and listened to me. She said to my mom, "Meg's sadness is her grief over the loss of her health."

DARNELL was my nurse at Baylor during the transplant. He was the epitome of cool. He worked the night shift. Seven at night to seven in the morning on the weekends. I would get excited on Friday around six because I knew I was going to get to see him. We talked about sports, Detroit—where he grew up, movies, and just life. It was great. When he came in to draw blood at three in the morning, I would wake up, and we would just talk. Darnell made sure I was in the least amount of pain as possible, made sure I was comfortable and always asked if there was anything he could do for me. The one thing that made him stand out from the others was that I felt safe with Darnell.

I feel certain that Angie, Angela, Judith, Darnell and all of my wonderful nurses were sent from above. They had so much love for me and all of their patients. These people made a difference in my life. They practically made me look forward to going to the hospital. I am grateful for them. I will never forget them. I am proud to say I know them.

All of these elements of medicine — technology, doctors, nurses — brought me back from the edge to another chance at a healthy life.

September 30:

Dang…tomorrow is October. Time flies, right? Now, is it flys or flies. I think "-ies" is plural for fly—bzzz…and "flys" is like "The kite flys north"…Whatever.

At the beginning of the day, oh-so-tired. Took a 3 hour nap today. Felt great. Saw Dr. Berryman. My counts were good. He did say that because I was not in complete remission, my chances of cure rate are 50%. Not bad, but not great, either. To me that sounds like 50% living, 50% dying. I know that's not what it means totally, but it kinda does. When someone does a bone marrow transplant and they are in complete remission, their cure rate goes up to 80%. Mom and I talked last night about the things that scare me. Yesterday, I was scared of the transplant. I know so many people survive, but some don't. Julie (on my intramural football team) told me about her sister's friend who had a transplant and passed away. YAK!

I'm scared of the Graft vs. Host thing. Lord, it would be really nice if I had as few complications as possible. I know it's my current situation, but I'm scared I won't be pretty again. I know I will, but the current environment does not help. I'm afraid of not meeting new people. Afraid of not going on dates and afraid of not having intimacy with someone. For the love, I'm so tired of being brave. I would really like a break from all of this and soon.

I have done absolutely nothing the past few days. I know I'm recovering, but geeze. I wake up at 11, eat, and take a 2 hour nap from 1 - 3. Now that my counts are up, I don't have much energy or desire to go anywhere. It's kinda sad I'm used to that. Actually, it's wonderful Mom and Dad are so great.

If we didn't love each other or couldn't stand each other, this would be pure hell.

Meg and Dad

Coach Conradt called today. It was nice talking to her. She invited me to do Race for the Cure in Austin. I told her I would be there if I had not started my transplant stuff.

I'm starting to feel better about the transplant. It still gets me that I still have cancer.

Oh, I want to live life. I want to do so many things. I want to help so many people. I want to meet so many people. I want to date. I want to kiss boys again. I want to dance, be outside, play ball, have a picnic, and, most important, not clean my groshong every night.

Good News—Grady Carpenter is cancer free. I think with testicular cancer once it's gone, it's gone forever. I'm so happy for him. He was so confident everything was going to be clear and he was right. God bless him.

More Good News—Mom and I are definitely going up to Chicago and Madison. I am so excited. I'll see Meggan, the Kohnens (her parents), her sister Katie, Josh who used to be at UT, the Oeths, and maybe a bunch more. It should be a great time. I'll be feeling good by then, and I'll be excited to get out of Arlington for a little bit. OK, my Xanax is kicking in.

Dear Lord,
Thank you for my life and my wonderful, loving family.
We all love you. Amen.

October 13:
Well, I'm in Arlington, in my bed, and listening to music when my plan was to be in Austin. Oh, how plans do change when you have cancer. I'll get to that in a minute.

Last weekend: So fun. Texas Football: Overrated. We went out to the West End Friday night. Not the best of ideas. All of Norman was hanging out at On the Border screaming TEXAS SUCKS. That is definitely a maturity thing. I know I used to be that ridiculous screaming OU SUCKS every 10 seconds, but I had my share when I was younger. Now, since I'm so mature ☺, it just looks silly. How long can you yell OU SUCKS and TEXAS SUCKS and get pleasure? Anywho, met up with Lara downtown and she looks great. Not cute. Pretty. Boys wanted her. We left there and went to Lower Greenville. It was a good time. Good group, too. Tracy, Melissa (Tracy's roommate and UT soccer player), Katie, Randa, Eryn, me. Afterward, we went to Taco Cabana. Katie almost got into a fight with 2 nasty old men who were using the P word. Gross. It makes me wonder, "Do those old, not so cute men think they're attractive and 23-year-old girls are going to want them?" Not so much.

The Game: We lost. That's all that needs to be said about the game. We're too cocky, not tough and, unfortunately, Chris Simms is not that good.

Why I'm in Arlington:
My friggin' toe is infected. Yesterday it got a little puss (then add a "-y"). I really don't want to write that word. It doesn't hurt at all just sitting here, but when I touch it— OUCH. So, I'm going to see Dr. Berryman tomorrow. Who

knows what he'll say? I have to get this taken care of before our trip to Chicago. If I have an infection going into the transplant, I'd be screwed. So we're getting this taken care of now. It's so frustrating. Nothing is ever set in stone except the damn doctor appointments. I'm so tired. I'm so jealous of other girls who look cute and are meeting guys. Jealous of people who don't have this shit to deal with. And now…I'm tired. I was planning on writing about 10 pages on my frustration. Guess not.

Last thing, I have the most wonderful friends. They are so sweet, caring, and, most of all, loyal. I love them so much.

October 17:

Went shopping today. I got some cute stuff which will probably be out of style by the time I wear normal clothes. Oh dear, when I tried my clothes on—not so cute. Even before cancer my belly was kinda big, but, at least, it had some muscle to it. Now, it's just big and gross. No, I'm going to go with absolutely disgusting. I look so forward to the day when I'm healthy, muscular, and people won't know what to say because I look so darn good. Today people say, "Oh, you look great." I know they are expecting this frail, deathly looking person. Well, I'm definitely not frail. I'm hoping this muscle thing isn't too far down the road.

Event for today: Got the toenail removed. Really not a big deal. The numbing shots burned a little, but that is normal. What hurt was this cauterizing thing. What does it mean to cauterize something? Basically, it burns like fire while singeing the capillaries. That didn't feel too good. Definitely could have done without that. I told the doctor it felt like my toe was burning and what do ya know? It really was. Sonofa.

Tomorrow, I meet with the radiologist. He'll probably tell me how much they are going to fry me. I look forward to that one. I'll also meet with Dr. Berryman and he should let me know about the date of the transplant. I won't be terribly disappointed if it's postponed until November 12. This would mean a few more weeks of feeling good, enjoying the weather, and I might get to Austin for Race for the Cure. If possible, I would really like to do that.

October 18:

Oh, the radiologist visit…that was uplifting. He told me the purpose of TBI (Total Body Irradiation) was to kill the bone marrow. This is why you have to get new marrow through a bone marrow transplant.

Here are some of the side effects he mentioned:
-Nausea and vomiting
-Fever
-Discoloration of the skin
-Lining of the mouth will become dry and irritated (mouth sores)
-Complete hair loss in about 2 weeks.
-Inflammation of the lungs
-Cataracts may begin to develop within 2 -3 years following treatment
-High probability infertility will result
-Early menopause in women

OK…can't really say I felt good about the visit. They could have lied and said stuff like, "Because we are frying your skin, you'll never have another pimple ever." or "Don't worry, once this is over you'll be prettier than ever before." Yeah, that didn't happen. Well, I can't worry about it. I can't control the side effects. All I care about now is going on vacation. Good times ahead.

October 23:

The Chicago Trip

Holy Cow! I've had such a good time. I guess I'll just try to remember everything. Meggan picked us up and took us to her place. We went to her volleyball game that night and the team she coaches, Northwestern, didn't look so good. They lost to Michigan State. Josh went out with us after the game and he is so damn funny. Seriously, the funniest guy I have ever met. Sunday, Bette (Justin's mom and Meggan's future mother-in-law) drove up from Madison to hang out with us. Bette, Josh, Meggan, Mom, and I headed down to Michigan Avenue. Huge Stores…Can't afford.

That night, Justin (Meggan's boyfriend) flew in from Ohio State law school to surprise me. That was so sweet. In summary: low key, but great medicine. I love seeing friends, meeting new people, and remembering good times.

Thoughts about the transplant: I feel better about things. I still don't want to do it, but I'm so ready to be done with all of this.

Last thing, how awesome was it to see everyone I wanted to see? Amazing. I loved every moment of it. And, I'm ready to do it again when all of this is behind us. Amen.

October 24:

We are currently at 20,000 ft and fat. Before we left, we ate breakfast with Meggan's family and again had a joyous time. I don't use the word joyous enough, do I? It was an A+ trip. I just look forward to doing it again when I'm well.

In other news—They think they have caught the sniper. If so, thank God. I can't even begin to imagine the fear those people felt. What the hell makes someone want to kill innocent people at hundreds of yards away? If they got the right guy, they also got his 17-year-old stepson. WHAT? 17 years old and having target practice with humans? Calling them bastards isn't harsh enough. It's total bullshit and they should rot in jail and get the shit beat out of them during their stay.

OK, one week from tomorrow is the transplant. I'm so ready to be done. This week, I don't think I acted any different than usual. I don't like that. This is what I want to feel... Care-free and enjoying every moment of life. I'm hoping that is the case after the transplant. With this looming, it kinda wears on you. It's not always on my mind, but I know I still have to do it.

Back to being fat—you know you're fat when you have permanent imprints on your belly from your belly rolls and your T-shirt. I am officially a tub of goo. Yes, goo.

About the weekend again—I love when connections are made. I got to see so many people I met last year and the year before.

Thank you, Heavenly Father, for this day. And, if they caught the sniper, thank you. Love you. Amen.

October 24:

My Ass! We are still on the plane. One subject I would like to address to finish out this journal and one I really hadn't thought about. I got cheated. I got cheated out of my last year of school. My last year was supposed to be basketball-free and oh-so-fun. I was supposed to party every weekend, get fat, kiss random boys, and live it up. Sure didn't happen. Fall semester, I didn't feel so hot and second semester I was gasping for air most of the time. No spring skiing. No trip to California. Nothing. It kinda pisses me off when I really think about it. This week, I listened to all these athletes talk about their final year without volleyball or their sport. I didn't get to do that. Yep, totally hacks me off. But I'm *going to use a year to travel and do my own thing—and, hopefully find a job.*

Places to visit:
Chicago—Meggan
California—Kim, Blake, Ally
Back to Cali—Holly, Tonya (UT friends)
Boston—Erin
New York—Sara (met her on my New York trip in 2001),Taryn
Idaho—Ms. Idaho (really Ms. Rainey, Meggan's grandmother)
Colorado—Brenda, Lindsay (at U of Colorado)
New Mexico—Brian M.
I would love to go to New Zealand or Australia. Oh, the places you will go.☺

My faith was my friend: my medicine and my strength. I understand that in our world, faith has a wide range of definitions. It could mean faith in a god or faith in Mother Earth or even faith that Oprah and Dr. Phil will come into your life and take away all your troubles. My faith rested in the hands of God. I turned to Him daily, thanking Him for the day, for my life, for my family and friends.

When I felt scared, depressed, and physically weak, I turned to Him and told Him my fears, my dreams, my gratitude and my plans for life. Because of my faith, I knew he was listening to me. This brought me peace and strength.

Various times throughout treatment, I would think about the tragedies which happened to people. I have never watched more episodes of CNN and nightly news than I did while I was in the hospital. Someone would survive September 11th and then would be diagnosed with breast cancer. A 23-year-old would be taking a road trip and be killed by a drunk driver. I heard story after story of tragedy and heartache. Thoughts surfaced such as, "If cancer happened to me at age 22, what else was going to happen to me during my lifetime?" When these thoughts crept into my mind, I would close my eyes and say this prayer:

And I said to the man who stood
    at the gate of the year:
"Give me a light, that I may tread safely
    into the unknown!"
And he replied:
"Go out into the darkness and put your hand
    into the Hand of God.
That shall be to you better than light and safer
    than a known way."
So, I went forth, and finding the Hand of God,

trod gladly into the night.
And He led me toward the hills
  and the breaking of day in the lone East.

—Minnie Louise Haskins, 1909

When saying this prayer, I would envision complete darkness. From this darkness, a hand would emerge, a strong, larger-than-life hand. This was the hand of God. I would place my hand in His, and he would lead me off into the distance. This prayer and vision brought me peace. It gave me strength and a sense of security. I knew that whatever happened to me, it was going to be OK. If I survived cancer, I would be OK. If I did not make it, I would be with Him and I would be OK.

November 1:

Two guesses on my whereabouts. Hospital or Hospital. Yes, I'm at the hospital. It's transplant time. Holy Cow!!! I was running around this morning like I was going off to college. First of all, Tracy came in last night. How stinkin' sweet! That was so nice of her and it was just a perfect visit. Tracy, Mrs. Starns (Mary Ann's mom), and I went to church to pray and talk to God. It was great. We prayed, read verses, and prayed some more.

So, here I am, back at Baylor and getting ready to do the transplant. I really don't know what I'm feeling. I'm back at the unknown again. Will I get this? Will I feel that? How long will this go on? Blah, blah, blah...So, I'm thinking I'm a little nervous. Sometimes I forget this little adventure is what will cure me—FOREVER, dang it. I must remember...it's about the transplant...it's about the cure.

Today, we got here at 2 p.m. I got a central line put in. Didn't feel too great. Numbing shot to my collarbone. OUCH! I'm getting fluids right now and will get chemo in the morning at 10.

Matt is doing great. He is up in Omaha, getting things together for his football camp. He is quite pumped about it. It really is amazing...he has absolutely no experience in interviewing or business stuff and seems to be doing great. His girl Megan came over last night, Halloween. Cool girl. She said she and Matt both talked about how they could be the one for each other. Whoa! I think I made her feel uncomfortable. Oops.

Mom and Dad are in good spots—I think. They said they were a little stressed which I really don't think happens to me.

143

This, for example, is something I know I have to do. This in is God's hands. I trust my nurses, my doctors, myself and I know it's not going to be my fault if something happens.

Dear Heavenly Father,

Thank you for this day and for my life. Thank you for all of my friends. Thank you for my wonderful family and all of the people praying for me. Give me physical, emotional, and mental strength. During tough times, let me lean on you and all of my supporters. Please be with James and all who know James as we pray he finds a match. Be with Christie and Brittany (Randa's friend just diagnosed with cervical cancer at age 20) during their difficult times. Bless these doctors with knowledge and precision. Love you and thank you. Amen.

November 2:

One Thiotepa (chemo) and 3 showers down, one more thiotepa and about 9 showers left. I have to take three showers a day to wash my "folds." Ugh! The chemo will stain my skin if the "folds" are not washed frequently. Folds—just a gross word. The doctors need to work on that.

Feeling good today. Got the room decorated thanks to Emily and her mom. They knew exactly what to bring. It doesn't look too dull in here any more. I watched college football all day today. Texas won. They beat Nebraska. Last team to beat Nebraska in Lincoln was Texas in 1998. Hook 'em. Mom and I walked about a mile today in the ward. Still feeling good. Still praying for Perry and his wife. (She had a transplant 10 years ago and has acute GvH now.) Until tomorrow.

November 3:

Day 3 at the hospital. I finished my last thing of chemo today. I'll get a few little doses of methotrexate, but nothing like I've gotten before. I was a little tired today because I got to bed so late last night. I had quite a few visitors today. Tomorrow is radiation. I'll be getting up at 5 a.m. to take a shower before the radiation. I have no idea what is going to happen. It's a little scary because of the unknown. But I can't feel bad too long because I have to get released, right? Damn Straight.

Dear Heavenly Father,

I face a new thing tomorrow. We are all hoping for the best possible results. Let's keep that up. OK? Good. Please let James get released from the hospital soon and let him find a donor. Thank you for my life today, my family, and my friends. Thank you for the success stories like Grady and Emily. Be with Emily on her CT scan next week. I love you. Amen.

Thanksgiving letter to my friends

Hello Buddies,

It's the night of November 3. I don't know how I'll be feeling in the next several days, but I wanted to get this all out before I start sleeping for days. During this holiday season, my family and I have so many things to be thankful for. I'm thankful for my doctors, nurses, advances in technology, and even chemotherapy and radiation.

You have shared my experience and you know what I'm saying when I say every day is a day of Thanksgiving. Each day I thank the good Lord for the day, my life, my wonderful family, my supporting, loving friends, and my blessed donor.

Y'all have no idea how much of an uplift it has been to

hear from you one way or another over the past 9 months. As you know, I've had some free time and the news can be quite depressing at times. Every day, however, I'm reminded of how many good people are in the world and how love is so healing to the soul. For that, I Thank You.

Blessings to you and your family during the holiday season. Hugs and Love to All.

November 4:

Finished two sessions of Total Body Irradiation today. I was pretty tired, but I don't know where that is coming from. Is it the chemo or the TBI? My stomach hasn't settled too much today. Mini-yak early in the night.

Confession: I'm scared of what the hell is going to happen. I don't mind feeling like shit. If I can sleep through it and eventually be done with it, then that's cool. So, I have 2 more days of radiation, then I'll get my cells, and let the games begin. I can do this. Hell, 8-year-olds can do this. Zac did this. It's time to buck it up and face whatever is going to happen.

Dear Heavenly Father,

Thank you for the day. Thank you for my life. Thank you for my donor, family, and wonderful friends. You and I will get through this together. I believe it. I will be searching for your hand in time of darkness. Let's get the best possible results. Thank you. Love you. Amen.

November 5:

One more day of treatment. Today, I had two radiation treatments. I feel OK. Pretty tired. Thrown up a couple of times. I get my cells tomorrow night or early the next morning. I should probably start ordering some medicine to settle down the stomach.

Dear Heavenly Father,
We are going to do this. One day at a time. We will get through this and we'll do it together. Watch over me and shine your light down on me. Thank you for this day, my life, my donor, family and friends. Love you.

November 8:

Day +2 post-transplant: As far as I can tell, things are going well. I've yakked a few times, got the runs, but that is about it. Holy geeze…my handwriting is horrible.

Apparently I'll be feeling quite lousy in the next couple of days. But HEY…There's nothing I can do about that. I don't think it can be worse than 106 degree fevers, swollen ankles, fainting in the shower—you get the picture. It might just last longer than the normal 3 to 4 days. I'll just ask for medicine and be on my way. This thing is almost over. I have healthy cells in my body. I'm cancer-free FOR REAL THIS TIME.

Whatever comes my way, I have to attack it. Throwing up isn't horrible. I always feel better after I do. Mouth Sores—really not too worried about them. I really don't think I'll get them. The times that will suck is when my counts drop way low, but they have done that before.

Dear Heavenly Father,

We are all hoping for the best possible results. I know there are enough people out there praying that will be the final outcome. Thank you for doctors, technology, advances in science, family, friends, strangers who have prayed for me. I love you. Amen.

November 9:

Day +3. Feeling good. I don't want to get cocky, but I'm feeling almost normal. My mouth is getting dry—super cotton mouth. I'm still wondering what the hell is going to happen. But I really wish I would quit worrying or thinking about it. Was the hard part doing the chemo and radiation or is it the Graft vs. Host thing? Hell, I don't know. But what I realized last night was I'm done with this shit. No more treatment—and it better be forever.

You know what I'm excited about doing? Going on a date. Just a date. Be wined and dined and end it with a sweet kiss. That's what I'm talking about. I'm so excited to think about running, buying new clothes, and going on vacation. You know, sometimes, I still think, "Holy Shit. I had cancer. I did 10 rounds of chemotherapy. I don't have any friggin' hair. Why do I have these cords sticking out of my boobs?" It's crazy.

Dear Heavenly Father,

Thank you for this glorious day. It sure "looks" pretty outside. Thank you for my wonderful donor. Thank you for my family and loving friends. Thank you for my life. Thank you for my doctors and the new technology. Please let everything with this process produce the best possible results. I love you. Amen.

November 13:

Well, Helloooooo…It's been a couple of days. It's not because I haven't felt well…I've just been so busy.☺ Day +7 of transplant. I'm feeling pretty good. No, I am feeling good. I'm really quite amazed with how good I feel. I don't want to get cocky, but I'm feeling almost "normal." The docs said I would feel pretty lousy, but not so much. My mouth has done awesome. It's sore, but no mouth sores. Celebrate good times…come on. The docs are quite impressed with how well I'm feeling. I love that. My counts have bottomed out. I got platelets yesterday and will probably need some more as well *as blood in the next several days.*

I haven't really had anything to eat in about a week. I just had some ice cream, but that has been it. It's not that I'm nauseated…I'm just not hungry. I've been getting food through my tubes and that seems to satisfy me just fine. The nutritionist said it would take about a month for me to get my appetite back. The only consistent pain would be the headaches. They aren't bad, but not so fun. Oh, and my feet do this tingling kinda hurt thing. That's from the f-ing methotrexate. For real, the person who founded that crap should burn in hell. But I had my last dose yesterday. No more chemotherapy will be put in my body ever again. I say that with confidence, but there is a tiny thought in the way back saying, "but, what if?" Crap. I don't think that made sense. But it really doesn't matter. Anywho…the point is I'm done with this crap. It's over. No more chemo. No more radiation. That's so exciting. I'm hoping the rest of things carry out like this:

In the next couple of days, my counts will start to come up. Oh, Happy Day. This means engraftment has taken place and the transplant worked. As little Graft vs. Host stuff as possible is the plan. Everyone seems to think crapping will not be a problem. I haven't gone for like 5 or 6 days. So, a little diarrhea and then I get to go home. So basically, as little discomfort as possible. That's not too much to ask for. Damn, my mouth tastes like shit.

Sad news—Emily's cancer has come back in her lungs. What the hell? I don't get it. Is this the hand she has been dealt? Get cancer at 15. Remove an arm. It spreads to the lungs. That's bull. Dear Lord, please put your hands on Emily. She doesn't deserve this. She has been through enough. Heal Her. Talk about inspiring. This girl had her shoulder removed and she is just smiling every day.

November 15:

Totally jinxed myself. Almost immediately after I called Katie and told her how good I was doing, I yakked. It was bile yak. So nasty. Then, to add to my jinx, I now have mouth sores. Son of a bitch, those suckers hurt. I don't even have them bad, but each time I swallow, the pain level goes from 0 to 9. It sucks ass. My lips are nasty chapped. But other than that, a million bucks I tell ya.

Awesome Story:

My pastor Reverend Robbins was teaching a Bible Study for about 150 adults. He was asked if he feels God's presence? He asked the class, "How many of you know Meg Brown?" Most of the people raised their hands. He said whenever I see Meg or talk to her, I feel God's presence. Holy Cow! Honored. Flattered. Humbled. What do you say to a comment like that? Oh, that's just the best compliment you could ever receive. Awesome.

Anywho, I've seen some action the past couple of days. Mouth sores, chills, still no crapping, feet hurting, headaches, yakking—good times. This sounds like a lot, but each thing hasn't been that bad. I've heard my mouth sores are nothing compared to some people's.

OK, 36 hours later, my throat still friggin' hurts. Painkillers help, but don't heal. I can deal with it. Only a few more days of it. Doctor Berryman is thinking my counts could come up in the next few days.

I got so much mail today. So fun. I have the best friends. Colorado Lindsay sent me a few Colorado scenery posters. Aunt Chick (Gram's sister) sent me a poster of Ohio State's football stadium. Erin's family sent a Boston Red Sox pennant and a New England Patriot hat. Kim sent a CD, but, most important, she sent me the best card. She is so funny. Love that girl. Mom hasn't been able to come up the past few days. She has had a scratchy throat. I think she is getting lonely and is pissed she can't be here.

November 16:

Day +10. Helloooooooo…Another good day so far. My mouth still hurts, but it's not bad. My legs are starting to ache. That is from the Neupegen. I'm trying to stay ahead by getting painkillers before it gets too bad. My white counts are still at 0. Platelets and hemoglobin came up and stayed up. That's what needs to happen. Dad has been with me since Wednesday. 4 straight days of me and Dad—and we have had a good time. He was so happy he was needed and he did great. I could tell, however, by the end of our quality time together, he was ready to go home. Going on walks seemed to be a hassle. Last night, he actually asked me if I really was hurting or if I was anticipating pain. What? Listen up, Dr. Asshole—are you really asking me (who has done 10 rounds of chemo and experienced 4 months of not breathing) if I'm anticipating pain? Get real. Other than that—good times. OK, I'm off to nap. Good nite.

November 17:

Today is a great day. My white blood cell count is on the rise. It's at 300 today. This means the cells have grafted. This means I don't have cancer. Hell, Yeah. I'm so pumped. Words don't even come close to describing it. Oh, I love it. Love Life. So now, we are waiting to see about Graft vs. Host Disease. I am hoping for a little skin irritation and that's it. You hear that upstairs? Just a little skin irritation. Thanks.

I have so much more to write, but I feel like I don't have time. Yeah, right. Tomorrow we shall write. Little tired.

Dear Heavenly Father,

Thank you for this beautiful day, my life, and my family.

Thank you for everything you have given me and blessed me with. I love you. Amen.

Until tomorrow.

November 18:

Before I go any farther, I have 1700 WBC (white blood count). I had 300 yesterday. Life is good. God is great. I love living. I'm so sorry, but I'm crazy sleepy. I have no idea why. Could be my lack of sleep last night, or my anti-nausea medicine, or the painkillers, or the low Hemoglobin, or my pure excitement drained out all of my energy. One of these is causing my eyes to shut. So, I'm going to stop this right now—good night.

November 21:

Wednesday and Thursday were days of rest. I've slept so much the past few days and vomited more than I would like to. I have started to eat more and drink more because that is the only way to go home. My mouth sores are gone. I think that spot on my throat is from throwing up so much.

Fun Story—My good friends Kim, her husband Scott, and Blake are hooking me up with a tour of California. It's going to be awesome.

I think I'll be going home soon because so many of the nurses have asked if I'm leaving. I wish.

November 24:

Day +18—The rumor is I'm heading home tomorrow. OK, I seriously have to crap every friggin' hour. Yesterday, I crapped my pants. Yeah, kinda gross. I think I have diarrhea-ed (past tense) 4 times today. Not good. Anywho, about tomorrow…I'm so pumped. No more hospital for me. Better not. Things have been pretty good. I got sick yesterday morning, but nothing today. I've been trying to drink as much as I can because I'll have to come back in if I get dehydrated. No thanks.

At this moment, my arms itch, my neck folds itch, and I'll probably have to go poop in a few minutes. Dr. Berryman said I might have some Graft vs. Host. The itching is a good sign and so is the diarrhea. Oh, and the other thing—I started my friggin' period. What the hell? Can we get a break? It's just nasty. Well, I gotta go. Gotta use it.

November 25:
HOME!

November 26—I think:

OH MY! Not your best day today. Let me give you the quick summary:

Diarrhea! That's it. I had it all day. Actually, it went like this. I woke up around 4 and didn't feel so good. "Oh, it'll pass." Not so much. 6 a.m.—go to the bathroom and yak. Great. Felt better, but come on. (DIA = Diarrhea)…Go to bed, get up, DIA, stand, sit, DIA, up, bed, up, DIA. Not kidding. Did this until 8. Go to the clinic from 9–2. Got fluids, f&*^ing steriods, went to the bathroom 5 times, and felt like complete shit. One time, I almost didn't make it. Scary. Oh my gosh—how embarrassing!! I seriously pulled my pants down and all of the fluids came with them. So nasty. So true. So, here we are at 11 p.m. Just got done taking my shower. How can I smell so bad when I sit in chairs and sleep all day? I guess that would be the 15 friggin' hot flashes. That was insane today. Hot, cold, sweating, need a blanket, want to stick my head in a freezer, need a fire. Not so fun…and smelly! WHEW!

So, what else happened today? Came home and decided

to eat some delicious apples. Again, smelled, felt, looked like apples, but my taste buds would disagree. Wake up from my 2 hour slumber and try more apples. Not bad. Almost yummy. Wait…why is my stomach doing that? OK…stretch it out. Take some Phenergan (HA! I have no idea how to spell that—the anti-nausea pill.) All right—got that down. Oh, not feeling good. Definitely going to yak. Sonofa. Go to the toilet and wait…wait…here it comes…SCORE…Oh, my apples. Seriously, if I lose my sense of taste, I should lose my sense of smell. If I can't taste the apples going down, why smell them coming up? At the time of projection (this is gross), all of my holes were working. I threw up, was having diarrhea, nose was running, and my cycle was in full effect.

I'm kinda proud my ovaries haven't totally caved in. I can't believe as much as I have cussed the menstrual cycle since 9th grade, I now embrace it. If I lose my fertility—whatever. But I really would like to keep some femininity. So, the bathroom adventure took me to about 7. I had multiple trips to the bed to stretch the stomach.

Dinner = 8 crakker—crap—I don't know how to spell crackers. Damn Chemo. Dinner = 8 crackers, chicken broth, and jello. Drank some pretty good fluids and didn't poop/ pee them out.

The current physical shape of the body—not so cute. My chest looks like a field of mice played ATTACK MEG'S BOOBS. Not cute. The rash is on the stomach and legs, but it's getting better. Atrophy everywhere. The face—ummm—could look better. The alien look is upon us. My eyelids or eyes are just simply nasty because there is not a strand of hair. My skin color was almost green yesterday. In conclusion, I look like total shit. I think it scared Mom a little bit, but tonight the skin tone is back to its normal pale. In conclusion, I look like total and complete SHIT!! Sincerely!

Happy Thoughts—Tomorrow can't be worse than today. It always seems when we are past the moment, it wasn't that bad. So, tomorrow will be better because that is just how the mind works.

Good Signs—I feel better tonight than I did last night. My diarrhea might be on the outs…not out of my ass, but Ba-Bye. That would really make me happy. My counts are better today than they ever were the entire month of October. That's what I'm most pleasantly surprised about. My hemoglobin was 11.6 today. I don't think it has been that high (except immediately after a transfusion) since this entire cancer thing started. It's so wonderful to have some energy. It's amazing what non-chemoed blood can do for you. That makes me think about the auto-transplant. I would think fatigue would be no comparison (meaning worse) than what it is now. If I were to put my old cells back in my body after being radiated? Thank you, Lord, for my donor and my other perfect match. Why? How come I have 2 perfect matches and 80 people just at Baylor right now are still looking for one? Thank you, Lord. Thank you, Donor. Thank you to whomever I'm supposed to thank. Life is so wonderful. I want to get back out there and live it.

Dear Heavenly Father,

Thank you for this day. Thank you for my life. Life is good. You are so good. How people live life without you or overcome mountains of challenges and tragedy is beyond me. Thank you for never leaving my side. I knew you were there all of the time. I know sometimes I talked to you when I was hurting. People say you shouldn't only call upon you when times are bad, but you make it so much better. Thank you. This is what I love…I love that there are billions of people in the world and millions are talking to you right now, but I feel at this moment it's ME and it's YOU. That's what I'm talking about. Thank you for that! I love you! Amen.

OK, the plan for tomorrow: I will wake up and my stomach will feel great. I will eat a few crackers and successfully digest my pills. Head to the doctor, get my drips, have few and far between trips to the bathroom (no trips would be splendid). Dr. Berryman will see the vast improvement in my rash while canceling the prednisone. I'll enjoy a pleasant ride home, take a nap, pee only, no use of any pink buckets, eat some crackers, laugh with Matt, take a shower, gag at my naked body, and get ready for Thanksgiving dinner which entails NOTHING since I won't taste anything. Sounds good. I'm out for the evening.

November 28

Happy Thanksgiving, INDEED! Not your normal Turkey Day, but a celebrated one. Dad and I hung out at the house and watched football and basketball. Cowboys won. Mavs lost. I woke up today at 11 to take pills and woke back up at 2:30 p.m. Nice. Oh my goodness—what I have to be thankful for?

> *—My wonderful loving family*
> *—My most loyal friends*
> *—All my doctors and nurses*
> *—My handsome, most precious donor*
> *—Technology and Medicine*
> *—Strangers who reach out to pray for others*
> *—Life*
> *—Love*
> *—Music, food, shelter*
> *—Most of all, I'm thankful for Faith. Where would so many of us be without it?*

Today, I got to talk to a few of my buddies: Eryn, Lara, Tracy, Brian M. I hope to talk to a few more tomorrow.

Tomorrow is another day at the doctor's office. It shouldn't be as long, but who knows? Today, I felt better than yesterday. I ate a little more and I think I moved around more. Actually, I felt good—just a little tired. So I'll end this with a prayer.

Dear Heavenly Father,

Thank you so much for this day, my life, my family, my friends, and for love. Thank you for my donor and somehow let him know he has done such a good thing and he saved my life. Tonight, I also thank you for taking care and watching out for my fellow club members: Emily, Grady, Brian E., James, Christie, and Brittany. I also want to say a little something for my girl Martha. I pray for her slow or speedy steps to recovery. Give her confidence and knowledge...she can do this. Send her love. Please continue to watch over me and we all pray for the best possible results. Send my love to all and hugs to Mamaw and Papaw. Love you. Amen.

That's all for now. Good night.

Chapter 22

December 2
– December 11, 2002

December 2:

Whoa, Nellie! First of all, it's December. Second of all, I'm friggin' tired. I got up around 12, ate something, and went back to bed for a couple of hours. I thought the steroids would be my hyper escape but not so much. I'm pretty tired at night and I have been having some dizzy spells. I don't think they are bad, but I don't think I should be having them. I go to the clinic tomorrow and get things checked out. My rash is better and I think the dizziness is going away. I walked for about 12 minutes today while hanging on for dear life to Mom's arm. It's so amazing that not even 2 years ago, I was running sprints, lifting weights, working my ass off and today walking at a snail's pace for 10 minutes is a struggle. Oh well—I'm alive.

Tomorrow, we are going to the doc's early. Charlie from church came over today and brought me a Chris Simms jersey. If I didn't make fun of people who wore those, I'd totally wear it. It was 50 bucks or something. Whoa! So nice.

So for my prayer—Dear Heavenly Father,

Thank you for my life and for this day. Thanks for good people like Charlie and Mrs. Talkington (church friend) who stopped by just to say hello. Today, I lift my club buddies up—Emily, James, Christie, Grady, Brittany, and Martha (even though she's in a different tough club). These people deserve their second chance like me. Love you. Amen.

December 4:

Whoa! Started out a little tired. I could barely keep my eyes open on the drive over to the clinic. Got there, got my

159

fluids, bone marrow aspirate, and we just got home. Same old report. My glucose is still quite high and I'm hoping the tapering of the steroids will help that problem. Still a little dizzy, not much of an appetite, but what's new? The nutrition lady suggested I eat about 15 servings of protein a day. My ass. Not going to happen right now. I need more protein because, AGAIN, the f*%^ing steroids tear down your muscles. Good to hear, fellas.

This time last year, I was curled up on the couch in pain because I puffed too much on an inhaler. Yeah, that day sucked. Mom and I were talking about those hellish days earlier today. Oh, the memories. OK, for real, I got to get some hobbies. Reading is a must. I'll be making my book list pretty soon. Pool—I could get good at that. Learn the Stock Market—Dad could teach some stuff. Dominoes and Blackjack—Dad again. Oh, the possibilities…spelling needs work, too. So, if I'm feeling better in a couple of days, I might get motivated. I always feel so much better when I see people. I have to do that in my life. I just get instant energy. Ok, that's all for now. Soon, I'll talk about dream vacations. Sarah came over for dinner. She's such a cutie.

December 5:

Another day of fatigue. First of all, I almost passed out at 4 this morning. Check that—I did faint. I didn't make it to the bed. Hit the floor after washing my hands and I started shaking. Little scary. F*&^ing Steroids. Bastards.

Today is a day of writing Christmas and Thank You cards. It's kind of nice to get something done. Who knows what the rest of the day will bring? Oh, the suspense.☺

I'm back. More about today—it was a good day. I had good energy. No nap. Wrote a ton of Christmas cards. Walked for 12 minutes on the treadmill at 1.5 mph. Look out!

And I've just taken some Lortab because I've got some pain in my legs. I think it's from my ultra cute slippers Matt gave me. Cute, but not big on support.

Anywho...Jennifer D. (two grades ahead of me at Arlington High and who lives in our neighborhood) came over today. She has Lyme's disease. She was a mess. She didn't look sick. She has hair, but, oh my, is she depressed. She's been at home for about a year. The doctors say they are 99.9% sure it's Lyme's disease. Here's the crappy thing— you aren't cured of it. She can only take antibiotics. She takes 60 pills a day. I'll quit bitching about my 20. She kept talking about how bad I must feel, my fatigue, and blah, blah, blah, but that girl is worse off than me. I've been through a year of hell and now I'm on recovery road. It seems like she hasn't really gone anywhere in her treatment. She has chronic pain, memory loss, and is just not happy. She said there is not enough research to find a cure. Damn, that sucks. At least with cancer, you have curing options like chemo, radiation, and transplants. She doesn't have anything. My thing lasted me a year and some months. Will her battle last her entire life? I'm hoping she can come over in the next few months, hang out, laugh, watch movies, and just forget about things.

Tomorrow is the doctor and tomorrow night Aunt Beth is coming over for Girls Night In. Should be fun. Until later—good night.

December 7:

Good day today and a fun night yesterday. Yesterday was the doctor. Same thing. Glucose level is still through the roof, but we hope reducing the steroids takes care of that. I woke up yesterday morning at 3. Thank you, Steroids. Took it pretty easy the rest of the day. SHOCKER! But last night, Aunt Beth came over and we watched The Graduate.

Little weird. Beautiful people, but they were so jacked up. I think it's so interesting how different generations have different thoughts and how they change. Mom and I had a little sleepover last night. It was so fun. I love her so much. She's my ultimate best friend. Today I slept in until about 12. Feeling rested. Addressed some Christmas cards, so I almost feel productive.

Oh my gosh—Emily Hunter—My Hero—made the varsity soccer team. She had to run a mile under 7:30. She ran it in 7:27. No training. She just had surgery to remove cancer from her friggin' lungs. She's amazing. Inspiring. Anything you want to call it—that's her. I'm so proud of her.

December 9:

Oh, Steroids—Gotta love them. Actually, I'm fading, so this will be shorter than anticipated. Just a day update. Mom got another checkup today. Good to go. My appointment went well today. Counts are good. A few aches and pains. Feet hurt and shins feel like I've run a marathon. Tingling in the feet and sensations are dulled. They are trying to come up with something, but I really don't think they have a clue. AND I stink. Seriously. 7th grade boy. Just got out of the shower and I smell. It's nasty. Is it the chemicals, my blessed European Donor, radiation? Who knows? But I smell. Other than that, things are good. Getting some tastes back. Didn't nap today (steroids) and talked to so many people: Blake, Jill P., Lara, Christie, Mary Ann. Emailed quite a few and wrote more Christmas/Appreciation cards. I really feel productive. Talked to Katie last night and she sounded great. Talked to Ally last night, too. Cool kid. She is real and she relates. I'm really excited about meeting her one day.

Yesterday, Matt and Megan came over. We watched the Cowboys suck it up in the last 6 minutes and blow the lead.

I think Matt and Megan have a good thing going. They are friends which is a first for Matt. I really don't see them breaking up. He said she makes him laugh. Another first: she is so comfortable with us and around new people. She has confidence, but isn't brash—another good quality lacking in some other women of choice. So, thumbs up for Megan.

Dear Heavenly Father,

Tonight, I lift up those who are in this tough club. About Jennifer—she deserves help and wants help. Open her heart, mind, and soul to You and the powers of healing. She's struggling right now and for good reason. Give her faith and lead someone to her with positive feedback. Watch over my hero Emily. What else can you say about her? She is amazing. Keep her cancer free today and every day for the rest of her long, healthy life. As for me, let's just keep on with what we are doing. I know you have your hand on me and are holding me up. I know you have big plans for me and you know how excited I am to fulfill them. Thank you for my second chance at life. Give Mamaw and Papaw a hug for me. Love you. Amen.

December 11:

Let me give you the glorious update.

4 a.m.—woke up to pee

5 - 7a.m.—woke up to pee

7 a.m.—get up for real

8 a.m.—leave for the doctor

9 a.m.—get fluids

12 p.m.—Dr. Berryman arrives. He is so giddy. He tells me that my bone marrow biopsy test has come back negative. I ask him what that means. He said, "Meg Brown—You are cancer free and in complete remission. Your old bone marrow is totally gone and your new bone marrow is working at 100%."

163

OH MY GOSH. THE BEST DAY OF MY LIFE. We knew he was going to say that, but to actually hear him say it—I can't even explain it. Mom and I went to the bathroom, hugged, and cried tears of complete joy. I called Dad—couldn't complete the sentence. Called Gramps—couldn't finish. Lara—same. Tracy—same. I called everyone in my address book and cried every time. I called people I didn't even know. They were so happy for me. Just about all of my friends cried with me. I'm so happy to be alive. The feeling is indescribable. So many people called today. I think I'm the most loved person in the world right now. I'm so grateful and thankful. I really don't know what to do. The plan is to still be careful, rest, and go back to the doctors. But my new bone marrow is working at 100%. That's so awesome.

Dear Heavenly and Most Wonderful Father,

Thank you! Thank you! Thank you! Thank you for my blessed donor. My wonderful doctors. My nurses. My friends. My family. Technology. Thank you for Life. Thank you for Love. Thank you for Happiness. Thank You for Faith. Thank you so much. I'm so happy. Love is so good and I can only hope people feel half as much as I have felt during this time. We did it. Praise Everything. Today and every day I lift people up to you who need you: James, Emily, Christie, Martha, Grady, Perry and his family, and others who are members of the tough club. Love you so much, Lord. Thank you and Praise You. Amen.

Oh, Life is Beautiful. I'm Cancer Free Today. My New Bone Marrow is 100% working and I'm in COMPLETE REMISSION. ☺

Meg and Dr. Brian Berryman after they finished
the North Trails Half-marathon, May 2004

DR. BERRYMAN is known to our family as The Man.
Dr. Berryman, bottom line, saved my life. Dr. Berryman is
knowledgeable, honest, loyal, passionate, sensitive, funny,
interested, and loving. Not only does he save lives as a
doctor, he also raises money for The Leukemia & Lymphoma
Society by running marathons for Team in Training. He
always made time for me and my trillion questions. He
always told me straight-up what the chances were, the
possibilities, his concerns, and what would be in my best
interest. One time when I asked him about another patient,
the news wasn't good. He said, "This is a tough club you
belong to." Since then I refer to my cancer friends as
members of The Tough Club. I enjoy seeing Dr. Berryman
not only because he tells me I am healthy, but because he is
a good guy and I enjoy talking with him. It's an honor to call
Dr. Berryman my friend. Dr. Berryman already did
everything for me.

Chapter 23

December 13, 2002
– January 16, 2003

December 13:

Another cancer-free day. Dad and I went to the doctor at 10 and got good news. Everything is looking good. Dr. Berryman said I'm doing the best he has ever seen. Ya-hoo!!! He also pointed out I have no muscles. Yeah, got that. For real, my calves are so not there. Thighs — not so much.

Today, my appetite was a little lower than normal. It's so weird to me. I don't feel like I'm going to be sick, but I just don't want to eat. I haven't lost that much weight. They expected 5% - 10% weight loss. That's really not that bad. What else with the health? Feet are getting back some sensation...don't hurt really, but almost like they are warming up from being in the snow. Skin is so dry. If I scratch myself, I tend to bleed. That's from the radiation. Fatigue was pretty good today. Lying down a lot and taking some naps.

Sad Story — Leah, one of the nurses, asked how things at home were going. I'm thinking, "Couldn't be better." She told my dad of a girl who showers 5 times a day to get some alone time. How sad is that? That's so opposite with how I feel about our house. I love being around my parents and I hug them every chance I get...at least that's how I feel right now. Geeze, that would suck if we didn't like each other. Why are we so lucky to have love like that and another patient is banging her head against the wall?

Dad is just so funny. It's so wonderful to see him living life, enjoying things and doing things. We have talked more about dumb, irrelevant topics in the past month than we have our entire lives. I enjoy his insight and I think he enjoys mine.

We are friends. We are off the father/daughter relationship thing. It's great. I know my success came from my attitude, but it's got to be from nurture, too. Even though at times he was stressed, he still knew what to do. It blows my mind to find out so many men leave their wives during treatment. What? How do you do that? Don't the vows say IN SICKNESS AND IN HEALTH?

I just took a sleeping pill.

The other day I got a newsletter from a friend who witnesses to college kids and is their mentor. Every newsletter asks for money. That's great and all, but I sure don't have it. In the pamphlet she sent, it talked about how we are living in sin and we are sinful people. I don't know about all that. I'm actually quite excited about the day when someone says to me, "Everything happens for a reason." This is where I say, "Yeah, I don't agree with that one anymore." Yes, I do think some things happen for a reason, but not EVERYTHING. It's such an easy response because people don't know what to say or think when bad things happens. People don't want to think God let something bad happen for no reason. Couldn't it be possible God doesn't do bad things to people? He is there for support, for comfort, to listen, and to love when people need him.

Tell me the reason for drunk-driving fatalities, unexplained deaths, children born with birth defects, cancer, rapes, cold-blooded murder, car accidents, natural disasters, September 11. There are no reasons because, unfortunately, bad things just happen. After a few more Kushner books, I'll have more insight.

But today was another glorious day. Oh, these mood swings.

Dr. Berryman told me I must lay very low for the first 100 days. There is no sense in taking risks. Schools are closing everywhere because of the flu. Don't need any of that.

Dear Heavenly Father,

Thank you again for this beautiful and glorious day. As you know, our house is happy. Thank you for your strength and guidance. Thank you for life and love. Tonight we lift those up who have to face what they don't want to or their fears. Oh, this pill is kicking in. I just want you to hold me and lift me up. I know I don't have any muscles, but if I could, I would return the favor. Thank you, God. I love you.

December 16:

HOT FLASHES!!! My head is soaking wet. Probably not normal. Check up on the Body: It's doing weird stuff. My vagina. Yes, I said vagina. It's not being so kind. It kinda burns when I pee and I have to pee a lot. They think it's a little tremor or something down there, but it pinches. Sometimes pleasurable ☺ but not really. Apparently, the muscles even THERE are weak and don't always hold in the pee. Good stuff. Today, I have felt like I have to pee and then I don't. I'm not concerned yet. It's just weird. My tests came back fine…so I'd think it would show up or something. The skin is so dry. I soak up the lotion. The neuropathy is not bad. Not painful, but not comfortable. I smell! So Bad!!! How can I stink when all I do is sit during the day? I'm talking take a shower and smell an hour later. When I mention this to the nurses, they seem quite surprised. That's comforting. It's weird—now that I'm healthy, I look the most cancerish. My face is so big. Bigger than it has ever been. My friends might be a little scared when they see me. I really don't understand the steroids. I know they help—somehow—but GEEZE they jack you up. They deplete your muscle, give you fake energy, give you a moon face, and they usually increase your appetite. Not here. Last year, it didn't do it, either. I have lost about 15 pounds since the day I checked in for the transplant. I didn't really think I would lose much weight and I thought I would have an appetite. But lately, I just have no desire to eat. I don't get sick, but I'd rather not. Not normal for the Brown Family.

Today, I took Josh—a new patient—the Chris Simms jersey. He loved it. He looked good. I think he is still in the state of WHAT THE HECK IS GOING ON! I don't understand. The more I think about how lucky and blessed we are I think about Perry's wife who died or people whose transplants failed. Why? I feel like I can't say "Thank You, Lord" enough throughout the day. I'm definitely in my own little world. So happy to be done with things, so grateful, and wondering how someone can't enjoy life. Lance Armstrong was right. Cancer is crap, but it will be the best thing that ever happened to me. I hope I never lose the feelings I have had over the past week. I want to feel like this every day of my life.

I think Mom and I are going by Mission Arlington to drop off some toys and stuffed animals. I'm also wanting to purchase an animal from The Heifer Project. They send animals to the poorest countries. These animals supply food, clothing, and nourishment for months—maybe even years. Saw it on Oprah. Pretty cool.

Last thing—Sarah had so much fun running in the White Rock Marathon. She did so good and she did it for me through Team In Training. I think it might have been a life-changer for her. She's going to do the one in San Diego this summer. She invited me to go. I should be able to walk a little by then. It will take a while, but how fun it will be to get some muscle and not pee on myself.

December 18:

One week until Christmas. Every day has been feeling like Christmas around here lately.

Health Update—Urinary viral infection and my line might have some bacteria in it. Dr. Berryman isn't worried about it. He said this is just part of it. I was happy to hear him say that. Today was pretty long over there. Left at 9 and got home at 3. I have to get infusions for 10 straight days and I think each day might be just as long. Who cares? You gotta do what you gotta do.

I have so many more things to say and talk about, but I'd be up until 4 in the morning. Oh, my feet are burning. Damn nerve damage.

Life is so fun. Every day—I can't even explain the feeling. I absolutely love it.

December 22:

Oh my! Let me tell you about yesterday. Clinic, yada, yada, had a good time. Got some good news about my fat face. I asked the nurse to rate my puffiness on a scale from 1 to 10. One, being beautiful bone structure and 10 being—SWEET MARY AND JOSEPH—YOUR FACE IS GOING TO EXPLODE. I'm a 4. Excellent news!!!

Around 4:30, Brian M. came over. He is such a good guy. We chatted about anything and everything. Watched the girls beat Tennessee by one. Hell of a game.

Prednisone disguising Meg's face

Then, Grady and his wife Leslie came over. Check this: Leslie knows someone in USA basketball. This someone knew about me and Grady. Well, somehow she got a framed picture of the USA Women's Basketball World Championship Team and an autographed **GAME BALL** *of the championship game. Are you kidding? I'm crying. I couldn't believe it. People are so wonderful. How are they so good? Oh, I don't know what else to say about it. Speechless.*

Grady, Leslie and I just sat around and talked basketball, treatment, and recovery. It's great talking to people who have gone through it. Grady just casually mentioned he had his testicle removed while I talked about birth control and boobs. I'm sure Brian was squirming in his chair. It was great.

Today, I get to see Lara. I'm going to squeeze that girl so tight and probably shed a few tears. I'm so excited. I feel so good. My legs ache pretty good by the end of the day, but the energy is up. I'm loving it.

December 23:
Another awesome day.
Dear Heavenly Father,
Lord, I have to admit…I get scared sometimes. I'm so happy right now. I don't want things to change. I know bad things happen and they just do, but, dang…I don't want them to. I know the odds are in my favor, but we all know things pop up. So, I'm going to continue to close my eyes and find your hands and trust in you. I'm sure you are happy to hear that. Oh, I love you, Lord, and we'll be chatting soon. Amen.

Meg and brother Matt Christmas Eve 2002

December 25:

Merry Christmas—Things here have been great. My yesterday was amazing. I woke up at 3 this morning and didn't go back to sleep. Did I get anything accomplished? No. Then, the visitors started to roll in. I cry every time I see somebody. My eyes are killing me. Oh, well. Matt came over about 4. He and I hung out while Mom and Dad went to church. Talked to people on the phone and the best was talking to Martha. She sounded wonderful. She couldn't really talk about her plans because I don't think she knows. She wanted to tell me how much our letters have helped her and inspired her. She shares them with her buddies. She sounds determined and she sounds happy. She said that. "I'm so happy." She knows it's about love and she feels it. It was so good talking to her. I know she can do this. She has to.

Matt and I talked for about 3 hours on absolutely nothing to everything. Sports, drinking, cancer, fear, sex, drugs, everything…it was awesome.

After church, the family opened presents. Of course, I sure didn't need anything, but I received a free plane ticket, yoga stuff, gorgeous earrings, sweaters, DVD of Friends, and some other goodies. Then, at around 9:30, the Starns Family came by to sing some Christmas Carols. Yeah, I cried. Actually, it was more like bawling. I hadn't seen them since I found out about my remission. A few of them had colds, so they couldn't come in. I wanted to bust through the window and give them hugs. They are such a good family. They feel like my family. The grandparents were there, too, with some fresh banana pudding—one of the best things in the world. My family ate half last night. Fatty. It was just a great day. My face hurts from smiling so much. I really don't think this feeling will ever end. I would really like to think of another way to describe it besides, "I'm so happy. I don't know how to explain it." Maybe if I write it out it will help. Pure Joy. Light as a feather. Carefree. Complete love for life. Grateful to God. Feel like He and I are brother and sister. I pray more because I know He is listening because I feel his presence. Euphoric. I always want to feel this way. I will. You know why? Because (break into song) BOTH MOM AND ME ARE CANCER FREE.

December 26:

Not a good day for others. Illery Sparks, one of the academic counselors at UT, was killed in a car accident today. The people in the car were Bev Kearney (UT track coach), Illery's 2-year-old daughter, a woman named Michelle, and Michelle's mother. Michelle's mom was also killed. Bev had back surgery today and they don't know if she will be able to walk again. Also, Emily Hunter got her scans back today and they found some more spots on her lungs. They are going to wait until January 13 to see if more have come up or if those spots have gotten larger. What the heck? Now, I know the deal with Em isn't good. But it doesn't mean she's done fighting. I know she is just tired. Damn...enough is enough. I hope Illery was happy and OK... meaning if something happened to me, I'd be OK with it.

Dear Heavenly Father,

You have somebody new up there today. She is a cool lady. Even though this wasn't the best news day here or in many other places, thank you for this day. Be with the Sparks family. Be with Emily and her family. Touch Emily with your healing hand. Lord, I just want everyone to be happy, healthy, and live to be 100. I know people go through crap like this every day. It just stinks. Please be with our leaders during this time and I don't even know how to pray for that. Bless our Soldiers. Thank you for continuing to heal and refresh me. Let's keep it up. And I have a prayer for my brain. I don't want to worry about things—like people safely arriving at their destinations. I just want them to get there and I have a tendency to think of not good things that could happen. I need to stop. I know that's not having faith and it's getting annoying. So, I will close my eyes and reach for your hand knowing it is there in the darkness. Love you and thank you for listening. Amen.

December 29:

Oh my—I have never been more tired. Worst hangover times 10. I had my best sleep night and I'm so exhausted.

Heavenly Father,

In remembrance—Perry's wife, Illery and her family, Michelle and her family, and the UT family. As for myself, I ask for continued strength, best possible results, and easing of the mind. I lift up our nation's leaders. They need you. Our country, of course, needs you. We can't just pounce on everyone. Let's negotiate or something. Ease our country's fears. I love you, Heavenly Father, and thank you for all the good in the world. Amen.

December 29:

Hello again. Today I wrote my letter to Oprah. It's pretty good. I really think I could get on there. We shall see.

Tomorrow, I'm going to the clinic early to get some fluids, magnesium, and some platelets. I take all of this magnesium, but then it makes me crap. Therefore, I lose all the magnesium. A little counterproductive.

January 1, 2003 (12:30 a.m.):

HAPPY NEW YEAR! GOOD-BYE, 2002.

Mom and I picked up Megan. She and Matt are so getting married. They are great for each other. We laughed so much. She's a funny girl. Morgen came over about 5:30. We just hung out and talked for about 5 hours. Morgen — How refreshing! She has things together. My friends are quite amazing. She's honest, confident, smart, sweet, and every man's dream. Every friend's dream. I'm glad I'm one of them. We hung out all night and watched the ball drop.

On the phone, I talked to Tracy from Times Square at 11:50. Also talked to Lara, Aunt Beth, Brian M., and Martha. Martha is so damn hilarious. I'm so pumped for her to "get out." All we do is laugh when we are on the phone. She got my letters and said she almost peed in her pants from laughing.

Dear Heavenly Father,

Thank you for this day. Thank you for 2002. I'm not kidding. You know it's done some good and will grow into greatness. And, Lord, I pray for my continued progress, success, and the best possible results. Please watch over my friends tonight. Guide them to safety. I know people are going to be idiots—just don't let them be idiots with my friends. Thanks! Also, we all lift up our nation's leaders and our soldiers.

My mom and I are cancer-free in 2003 and every following day that be. That's kinda catchy. I love you. Amen.

January 5:

OH MY GOSH—could not be more tired. Totally wiped out.

Contributing factors: 3 hours of sleep Thursday. Katie came over last night and spent the night—6 hours sleep. Yesterday, Dad and I walked about a mile and a half. Yeah, not so smart. That was so dumb. My legs were fine while we were walking because I can't feel them. But today, my back is a little sore and my would-be thighs are hurting. My eyes are having trouble staying open. But I just talked to Martha and she "gets out" soon. The latest will be February 18. Damn, she is funny. She's refreshing to talk to, and I can't even imagine what her day-to-day life is like. Meeting after meeting. Talking and more talking. Doing things you would never fathom doing. Both of us went from Division I athletes to having bodies of complete mush. Crazy Indeed.

Let me fill you in on yesterday's walk. Dad asked what is next. I told him Oprah. I'm not kidding. I really think I can get on it. Dad asked about the video script I made for it. And I knew it would be better if he read it instead of me verbalizing it, but I went ahead. Hoping Dad, who isn't into new ideas, had changed in that respect and would listen to the idea and be excited—not so much. I said I agree with Lance when he says, "Cancer is the best thing that has ever happened to me." Dad mocked me, made a sigh, and rolled his eyes. *Now, I know that statement is a bit shocking, but that is how I feel. I guess I could say instead, "The result of having cancer has been the best thing that has ever happened to me."*

While Dad and I were walking, I got pissed. How could he not say our family is different? I told him I'm so proud I beat cancer and I will be proud every day of my life. I talked to Mom about this later…open the flood gates. I know part of it was fatigue, but I was really upset. Mom said she would have done anything for me to be where I'm at today emotionally without the cancer route. That's a good call, but that's not what happened. Cancer happened. It changed my life. No one knows how I feel. No one will ever know. Dad is trying to learn how to live each day. I'm pretty sure I know how to. No, I do know. I need to be careful not to be too "preachy" about how wonderful things are. Dad and I talked today. He's really good at expressing things, unlike a lot of men. He recognizes where I'm coming from, but he still has no idea. He apologized.

When Mom and I talked yesterday, we came to this conclusion: I want people to have gotten something out of this like I have. I want things to be different for people. But I have to realize they haven't gone through what I've gone through. We are not in the same spot.

I've just decided I'm not going to tell anyone else of my plans. People really don't seem to believe. I mention Oprah and I get the "Right, right." I'm going to write a book. "Right, right." Well, People, I think I have a legitimate shot at getting on Oprah and my book has awesome potential. So kiss my ass.

Mom and Me are cancer-free in 2003 and every day that is meant to be. Say What!!!

January 6:

Quite tired today. Damn that walk yesterday. I'm currently at the clinic getting some magnesium. I was a little jittery today. Parkinson's jittery. That's annoying. I don't think I mentioned this yesterday and I meant to. Doug B. battled leukemia for 11 years. He had a transplant one month before me. He called one night to inspire me and encourage me, but I think I had more energy than him. That's not the point. He wanted to see his little kid over Christmas. Well, now he's in the friggin' hospital with viral meningitis. What? What a bunch of crap. I almost threw up when Mom told me. I guess I'll be wearing a mask until May. My ass is not going to be set back. So today I pray for Doug.

January 7:

Sonofa—I'm back at the clinic. Spiked a fever last night. 101.3°. And my head friggin' hurts. My hands are still Parkinson's jittery. Here's the deal: The one day I mess up and take my Pro-Graf pill in the morning (not supposed to), my Pro-Graf level could possibly be out of whack. Convenient, you dumb ass.

January 8:

Today, I'm a bitch. Not in the best of moods and I'm tired. I could fall asleep in two seconds if I shut my eyes. I've been sleeping all day. I could go to bed right now. I got some things going on. A little rash and occasional fever. Loss of appetite. Today is one of the first days that I said this process is getting tiring. I'm starting to notice more aches and pains. I know this fatigue thing will level out (it better) but, geeze.

Other News—Our Country—We are about to go to war... and we really don't know why. George has said it's because Saddam has weapons of mass destruction. He does.

Saddam is an evil man. He gassed 100,000 of his own people. So, we send the U.N. over to Iraq with a 20,000 page document to check out these weapons. We know he has them and we don't want him to use them. We're searching. We're searching. WE CAN'T FIND THEM. DAMN. Bush continues to use the Fight Against Terrorism pitch which should definitely be one of our priorities. But Saddam wasn't the guy. It was that f*%$ing Bin Laden dude. Oh yeah, we can't find him, either. DAMN. The only thing said that has been consistent and accurate is Bush continues to say, "Saddam tried to kill my Dad." Now, I know that might not be the only thing, but you can't bring in personal crap when you are dealing with one of the most evil men ever. So Hum-de-dum...North Korea has nuclear weapons and doesn't like us, either. Rumsfeld: "We can beat up 2 countries."

What is the matter with us? I think we have started negotiating and they are actually going to sit down and talk. Yes, we are a powerful country. Yes, we can do things other countries can't do. But we don't always have to be the tough guy. We can show a little finesse. At the current time (I think this is what is going on), we are sending troops to Iraq, talking to North Korea, fighting terrorism, promoting a tax cut, and really no one knows what the hell is going on. George did a great job after September 11. He probably was perfect for America like Rudy was perfect for New York City. He's a good man and he's likable. But he is so stubborn. He's got that Texas arrogance. If you're not Texan, you're not good enough. I just don't see him as a big compromiser. The Democrats are sucking, too. They don't seem to stand up to much about the war. People are afraid if they say anything, they will be accused of anti-Patriotism or not caring about the fight against terrorism. Bush is always going to use September 11th and anti-terrorism as his pitch. It would be nice if we did something about it. Is our country really safer since the attacks? Some cockpits are armed. They are now personally screening all passengers—from 5-year-olds to 95-year-olds. Yeah, 5-year-olds carry bombs. I don't know if we are safer. It's scary.

Oh, for the love, 8 hours and 15 minutes at the clinic. That's a new record.

My body is in a hell of a shape right now. Did I mention my wrists went out on me the other day? Tonight, I looked down at my knees and they were abnormally swollen. Like hanging off to the side swollen. Definitely odd. My skin is so dry, but we think it's getting better. I have 2 giant old blister markers on my heels. They don't hurt...they are just gross. So basically, I'm growing tired of lotioning myself 2 - 3 times a day, taking 12 magnesium pills, not really knowing what to eat because I have no appetite, going to the clinic.

Next Topic—Mom and Dad are going to the country this weekend. Mitra is going to spend the night. Quite pumped about that. Those two can be alone and vent about me. I can be alone and vent about them. Even Mom needs to simmer. She's seemed a little edgy lately, and by 8 o'clock she is ready for bed. So, this will be a good, healthy break. And I'll get to share with Mitra LIFE WITH THE PARENTS WHEN IT'S NOT YOUR CHOICE. Seriously, thank God, we like each other.

January 11:

OK, Recovery Sucks. Seriously—what is going on in the body? I'm so damn tired. Slept 16 hours last night. Still tired. Stomach feels weird and my damn hands keep shaking. If I told my body to poop, I think it could. Who can do that? I believe I'm feeling the side effects of coming off the steroids. During Rounds 1, 3, 5, 7, I would be in pain because I would *just immediately stop the steroids. Now, we are going to drag it out and feel like ass for a long time. If it's the steroids, I can deal with this. But I feel sorry for anyone in my path. Tend to be a bit bitchy.*

On Thursday, we got news that Doug passed away. It's definitely a Tough Club and one you don't really want to be part of. That's all I have to say about that.

Mom and Matt are in the country. Mom was losing her marbles. It was going to be Mom and Dad in the country — me and Mitra at the house. Well, Mitra got sick and I pulled this steroid crap, so Dad is with me. He is so funny. He told me we don't have to see each other, but if I needed anything, let him know. Love him.

January 13:

For the love of the land…Let me set up the scene: I'm in the clinic. Tired? No, exhausted. Really don't know what the deal is. Is it coming off the steroids? I really thought I would need blood to boost the energy, but I don't. Right now, we've got two cubicles next to us blaring their damn televisions. They are watching Mama's House. Funny show, but I could think of something better. It's a little insane here today. Back to me. Why the hell am I so tired? Geeze…I could sleep all day. I nap, wake up, nap, do nothing, nap…go to bed for the night. I fall asleep within seconds. It would be nice if I felt some energy after my nap — not so much. I would talk about my exciting day yesterday, but all I did was watch football and sit on my ass.

OK, I'm going to bitch. This is getting old. My excitement I had about a month ago anticipating visits to the clinic is totally gone. I don't know when this fatigue thing will go away, but it's getting on my nerves. I'm on day 68 past the transplant, but it's been more than a year since all this started. Basically, I'm tired of this shit and I want to be done with it. DAMMIT.

January 16:

It's Thursday and I'm in the Vacation room (that's what we call Matt's old room. It has all my posters of the places I'm going to visit on my Victory Tour) watching Will and Grace. I have turned a corner. Monday—felt like butt. Tuesday—Feeling better. It was nice not going to the clinic. I was able to rest up. Wednesday, I went to the clinic for 6 hours. Dr. Berryman said I was doing well. He's pleased that my platelets are going up on their own. He said people whose platelets are puny, don't do so well. SCORE!

Today was a good day. Did my Oprah video today. I think it's pretty good.

JOSH was the only transplant patient I met younger than me. He was diagnosed at 18 with myelofibrosis in September 2002. He was kept alive with blood transfusions until they found a match. He had his unrelated donor transplant six weeks after mine. For the three or four months following our transplants, Josh improved faster than I did. But in April of 2003, just as my recovery really started to kick in, the whole thing crashed for him. He began suffering one complication after another. He has returned to the hospital numerous times. In October 2003, he was in the transplant unit's ICU and on a ventilator. He almost didn't make it. He has had multiple surgeries—on eyes, heels, shoulders, hips, spleen. He has never been completely off prednisone since his transplant over three years ago. He has regular rehab sessions to try to regain the strength to walk.

When I walked my first half-marathon for **TEAM IN TRAINING**, I walked in honor of Josh. Since early in 2004, Team in Training has provided me my main outlet for exercise. Team in Training is one of the largest endurance groups in the world. It raises money for The Leukemia and Lymphoma Society while participants run or walk half or full marathons. Participants also compete in triathlons and century rides (100 mile bike rides). The Society covers all blood-related cancers, including multiple myeloma. Since Sarah did a half-marathon for me and introduced me to TNT, I have completed 4 half-marathons. I did my first in 2004 and will finish my fifth in June 2006. Because my friends and family want to support me and my goal, I have raised over $20,000 for the society. I have had the chance to compete in San Francisco, Maui, and San Diego.

I believe in Team in Training because of its purpose and because of the positive people involved in the program. I believe in Team in Training because every competitor makes the team, joining together and raising money to find a cure.

Dear Ms. Winfrey,

I have an idea for your show. How about a fashion show for current cancer patients? The models and the audience members would be cancer patients currently undergoing chemotherapy. They could model different wigs, scarves, hats, bras and bathing suits. This would show people that cancer does not mean SIT AT HOME, WASTE AWAY, AND WAIT FOR REMISSION. Life does not stop because we have cancer. We celebrate life everyday and is there a better way to show this celebration than with you? I just think it would be simply FUN for people who are meeting challenges daily to strut their stuff and their style during a time in their life that will change them forever.

I probably would not have thought of this fashion show idea if cancer had not swept through my immediate family. On February 20, 2002, I was diagnosed with non-Hodgkins lymphoma—a month before my 23rd birthday. After four months of fighting an allergy diagnosis and reaching the edge on several occasions, I found out I had cancer—six months to the day after my mom was diagnosed with breast cancer on August 20, 2001.

We both had CT scans on February 20, 2002. Hers showed no cancer cells anywhere. Mine showed a 7.5 inch tumor wrapped around my trachea and that big vein that transports blood from the face to the heart. (I think it's called the Superior Vena Cava.)

The reason for my writing this is I wanted to express the idea that although cancer can be fatal, it doesn't have to kill your soul. My mom beat cancer with style and grace, and I feel like I am following in her footsteps. On your show, a common theme is FINDING YOUR SPIRIT. Well, cancer patients and survivors are forced to find their spirit. Because the idea of life and death has moved to the driver's seat, we realize our passions. Like those people in the fashion show, we have continued to fight and to realize how precious life is.

To share with you the history of my battle with cancer, I am enclosing an article that was printed in the Austin American Statesman in May.

If you decide to use the fashion show idea, neither my mom nor I could participate. She is in remission and my chemotherapy treatments would not allow me to travel. I'm sure the many cancer patients in the Chicago area would be more than happy to fill the bill.

Yours truly,
Meg Brown

January 22:

Great Day! I'm recovering. My counts were so good today. Dr. Berryman was so pumped for me. I don't have to go back until next Wednesday. I'll get my scans done and another bone marrow biopsy because it will be 3 months after the transplant. Whoa! 3 months. I don't know what I'll do in my spare time, but I'll figure something out. I almost feel weird about getting better. I haven't been on this side of the fence in a long time. Since October 2001, this is the first time a man of medicine has said really good things about me and told me I'm getting better. That's a long time.

Mom and Me are Cancer Free and loving it in 2003.

January 24:

Today was a complete sit on my butt and soak day. I did absolutely nothing. Woke up at 12, took a nap at 3, got tired around 4, and watched TV until 10. I talked to quite a few people on the phone, so that was nice. Last night, I talked to Ally Ross. She told me about a guy she met who lost an arm in a boating accident. It was inches away from being fatal. She met him while snowboarding. He said he has had 12 bonus years since that day. What a cool thing to say. I'm going to adopt or steal that saying. These are my bonus years. I was one week away from dying. That damn tumor was going to kill me. So now, I've got my bonus years going.

Current Problem—I don't feel so good. Little annoyed. I was on such a high after December 11, feeling so at peace, and happy…yada, yada, yada…now I feel like I'm back taking days for granted. I'm hoping it's because I don't feel so hot, and I'm going to blame this on the steroids. I just want to feel productive and not "waste" the day which has been given to us. I wasn't a punk before all of this happened, but I want to be different after this. Bottom Line—I'm tired of this recovery crap. I want to be recovered.

Dear Heavenly Father,

Thank you for this day. Thank you for my bonus days and my recovery. I think I'm needing a little bit of patience. I've been thinking about things down the road when I should know—We've only got today. I lift up Emily—give her strength as she recovers from her surgery. Please let this be it for that girl! Christie—let this new medicine shrink her tumor. May someone register for the bone marrow donor program who is a match for her. We all pray for our country and our soldiers. Lord, I don't know if I'm allowed to do this, but **PLEASE**, if something could happen to Saddam—like CANCER—and a really fast one, it would really be appreciated. Thousands of innocent people won't die, our country won't be in limbo, and maybe George can get over this "He tried to kill my dad" thing. Thank you. Love you. Amen.

January 27:

Brian M. asked me the other day if I thought we were running out of things to talk about. I think he thinks I'm losing interest in talking to him. Not the case. I'm friggin' tired. Emotionally, Physically, Mentally—I'm tired of it. I'm finally tired of talking about it. "Well, I'm getting better. I'm just fatigued because of these steroids...yada, yada, yada." That's all I have to say. I hate trying to think of things to say to Tracy. I didn't like the feeling I had with Kim. I hadn't seen that girl in 8 months and I felt like we were running out of things to talk about. I get tired thinking about talking on the phone for more than 15 minutes. I need to tell Brian to be *patient. I know he's wondering what is going on and if I'm OK. The critical part is over (I think). Soon, I'll be doing things. I'll have some more personality in my voice and I won't be so damn boring to talk to. The last thing I want him to think is that I don't I want to talk to him. It's not just him, it's anyone. I want Brian in my life. I want someone to talk to and someone to get to know. Unfortunately, that takes energy which I seem to be lacking at this juncture.*

Good news about Martha—her mom is taking a car to her on February 13. She said Martha is doing well and is going to be living at a halfway house with 3 sober women.

Please Lord, help Martha live her life.

February 1:

Today at 8 a.m. the Columbia Shuttle exploded as it entered back to Earth. It had been gone for 16 days and the families were waiting its arrival at 8:16 a.m. It exploded right over us—North Central Texas—and they are finding debris in the Nacogdoches area. Unfortunately, they have also found remains. 7 people were on board. There is really nothing to say about it. You want to know why and all you can do is pray for the families. Barf.

What's been going on in my crazy life? Yeah—about that. I haven't felt as tired this week as I did last week (as I journal at 8:45 p.m. in bed—about to go to sleep). I've gone walking the past two days and walked pretty fast. Little sore which kinda excites me. What am I not excited about? My stretch marks. Not so cute. Thank you steroids—AGAIN. Got them on my boobs, my butt, my love handles. They are gross. But what are you going to do? Who knows how many times my skin will stretch by the time I'm "normal"?

Matt and Megan came over tonight. Always a good time. Mom and Dad are going to the country and I'm going to chill

*at the house. It is supposed to be beautiful outside tomorrow.
I can work on my tan.☺*
Dear Heavenly Father,
*I hope everyone is praying for the families of those lost
today. Let them feel our love during this time.*

February 3:

*Got an email from Aunt Beth tonight. She said she had
been working on a plan to get me up to New York for the
summer. I guess I told her at one time I would love to spend
a summer in New York. Aunt Beth knows somebody who
could possibly get me a job with the New York Liberty.*
First Reaction — How awesome is that? NYC. Summer. Job.
Second Reaction — What about my travel plans?
Third Reaction — I can travel before the summer.
Fourth Reaction — I'll miss Mom.☺
*It's amazing how that piece of news sparked my energy
for about 2 hours. But now I'm tired again. Time for bed.
Seriously, I have only been up 9 hours today.*
Dear Heavenly Father,
*Thank you for this day and another bonus day for so
many people.*

February 7:

*Scans were clear. I really wasn't worried about that.
Done with the steroids. Today sucked. Got up at 11 and back
in bed from 1 - 4. Went to the Vacation Room for the rest of
the day. I get so dang tired the days after I drop steroids. I've
been saying this since November, but I think every day I
should start to feel better.*
*Our country was on high alert today. What does that
mean? What are we supposed to do? Get really scared or
really, really scared? We are about to go to war which isn't*

easing anyone's mind and North Korea, as well as several other countries, hates us. Not the best of times right now as far as feeling safe here or overseas.

Oh, pretty much not going to NYC for the summer job. Dr. Berryman thinks it would be too much too soon. He's right. I would also have to get a doctor up there and if something happened, I would want to see Berryman. But maybe next summer and I'll definitely vacation up there this summer. Oh yuck—don't want to write anymore.

February 12:

Made it over another bump. Since Friday, I have pretty much felt like crap. Sleep all day, diarrhea in the morning, and Monday I puked. Don't eat for the rest of the day, puke in the morning on the way to the doctors, and I gained 2 pounds. What the hell?

Here's the deal:

I have a bacterial infection and they are going to check and see if I have a viral infection. In order to do that, they will need to scope me down the throat and up the butt. Should be fun. I'll let you know how the 2 enemas turn out beforehand. Dr. Berryman said this is a very minor setback. I have to continue to focus on the most important thing: I got a report of clear scans and I'm Cancer Free and in Remission. Other news—Our Country. Holy Cow, it's scary. Bin Laden came out with another tape that basically said kill any American. He didn't really admit that he was with Saddam, but Bush thinks it's proof and is probably more determined. The CIA thinks it was a signal to launch other terrorist attacks. Bin Laden mentioned suicide bombers. SHIT! Homeland Security sent out a pamphlet or something which instructs people to have a plan if they were to separate from family. Buy duct tape to seal off doors and windows and buy bottled water and food that could last up to 3 days. What the hell? A group of kindergartners could have made up that. So, our country is scared, we are about to go to war, the economy blows, gas prices are sky high, and North Korea said they have a missile which could hit California. Not safe and secure times in the U.S. right now.

Dear Heavenly Father,

I come to you tonight with gratitude and a little bit of fear. Thank you for this day. It's so nice to be feeling better. I lift up our country. Please give whoever needs it the knowledge to stop any terrorism. Excuse my language, but please don't let our government piss off anyone else. Lift up our soldiers with brave hearts and strong bodies.

I lift up the club members: Emily, Josh, James, Christie, Belinda (a lady from church diagnosed with lung cancer in August 2001), Grady, Ally, her mom, Brian E. and Mom. And Jennifer and Martha. Thank you. I love you. Amen.

February 22:

One year. I have been undergoing treatment for one whole year. I had no idea on February 22, 2002 I would still have no hair and I would still be having shitty days one year later. I have felt like ass the past week. I took a break on Tuesday night, Wednesday, and Thursday, but before and after that, I haven't felt too smooth. First of all, in the past 6 days, I've had 3 minor procedures or surgeries. I have gone to the clinic 9 out of 14 days. I've gone every day this week.

*Friday, February 14, I started the morning with two enemas. Uncomfortable and quite degrading to sit there naked, sticking something filled with water up my butt. Those procedures (the scopes from mouth to butt) were fine—No Graft vs. Host in the stomach. Apparently, I have the best stomach they have ever seen. Thank you. **Tuesday** —I had a*

PICC (peripherally inserted central catheter) line put in my arm. No big deal. Not that painful, but it added to the longevity of the day. Those two days we spent about 10 hours at the clinic each day.

Wednesday—Removed the groshong. Glad to have that out. So, now when I take a shower, I cover half my arm and half my chest so the PICC line doesn't get wet. Just add that area to the skin irritation list.

This weekend I was supposed to go to Austin. Been thinking about it for 3 months. We decided it would have been too much to make that trip. Good thing. Last night = No appetite and felt like ass. This morning, threw up breakfast, big stomach cramps, and quite exhausted.

Dad and I talked a little bit today. He said he finally understood things. He thought after day 100, I would feel great. He thought that is what everyone else thought as well. Not me. I knew it didn't work that way. I vented on him a lot today. Basically, I told him I don't enjoy talking about cancer all of the time. I know it's my life right now, but I hate contemplating why I don't feel well. I told him I really don't like it when asked how I'm doing 3 times a day by the same person—that's him. I hope I didn't hurt his feelings. All he wants is for me to be well and happy.

Sometimes, I think if I'm not feeling well, I have failed. Today, my nurse asked me about coping/depression and today was the first day I hesitated. If I had said something, cancer would have gotten a point. I get knocked down a lot easier than I used to. When something like an infection or a bad day came up, I used to not even flinch. But now, I get knocked down and it seems to take me longer and longer to get back up. I haven't exercised in 2 weeks. My legs are so tight. I know most of that is the fluid, but I think some of it is the lack of exercise. In conclusion, the big stuff is fine. It's the *little things upsetting me and driving me crazy. I know there are going to be good days and bad days, but I would really like a string of a few good days. Tomorrow, I have off from the clinic. I'll probably sleep a bit tomorrow and try not to be sick. Until then…*

March 2:

Tomorrow, I'm going to speak at Randa's school. 350 people…don't know what I'm going to say…Yikes.

Not good news—My dentist Dr. Bauer has lymphoma. It's a slow growing kind. He had tests done and could have found out in December, but the doctors screwed up. They don't know about treatment yet. Crap!!

I got a letter from my donor yesterday. He wasn't allowed to sign his name, so he signed it, "Your Twin." Seems real nice. I'm so glad he wrote back and wants me to continue to correspond.

March 4:

I gave my first speech last night. Not great, but not bad. I think I ran my thoughts together and sounded confusing. Definitely room for improvement. Today was a rest day for the most part. I'm up to .75 miles on the treadmill. I'm not sure how good that is, but I'm not complaining about not being able to do more. I get a little tired. Going to the doctor tomorrow. I'm thinking I'm normal, but who knows?

March 9:

Feeling pretty damn good! Went to lunch with Mom, Gram and Gramps. Thursday I spoke at Coach Sager's girls basketball banquet. (I played under Coach Sager for AAU Team Texas in 1997.) This speech was better than the one on Monday. I feel girls will get more out of my speeches than boys. I thought I did well, said what I wanted, and got paid.

March 17:

I have kinda slacked off on my journal entries. I guess that's a good thing. That means I don't sit around all of the time thinking of things to talk about. Let me re-cap the week. Thursday, Lara came over. We went to the Big XII women's basketball tournament with Tracy and Randa. Saturday, we went to the championship game. The girls beat Tech. I got to go down on the court and hug the girls and the coaches. I'm very happy for Coach and her squad.

Other news—We are going to war. For sure. G.W. addressed the nation today. Told journalists to get out. Terror alert has been elevated to HIGH. Lord, please protect our soldiers and our nation from terrorists. Let this war be quick with few casualties. Saddam and his two sons have 48 hours to get out. CRAP!

I don't know much else. My hair is looking good. Can't tell if it's going to be straight or curly. Oh, my rash might be Graft vs. Host. But Dr. Berryman said people who are cured forever usually have a little GVH compared to those who don't have any.

March 19:

Shit! We are officially at war with Iraq! Is there always going to be war? Why do we continue to repeat history but with bigger and better ammunition? I really don't understand how war is the appropriate answer. Do we go against North Korea when they start talking trash? I heard the Bush Administration was planning on doing this before September 11th even happened. Why? Why do evil people like Saddam, who punishes people by raping them, even exist. People who burn their own citizens. What a bunch of bullshit.

People talk about how different things are today than they were back then (whatever time period they are talking about). Well, that's a crock. Back then, people did drugs, there was prostitution, parents sucked, young kids did horrible things, and in every era there has been war. Things that have changed—Civil Right, Women's Rights, attitudes toward the elderly, minorities and the disabled. But when there is a problem with another country, what do we (the world) do? We kill—just like the 1940s, 1800s, 1400s, and so on back through time.

That's crap. What have we learned from September 11? We were so united for a few months. So many people who believe "Everything happens for a reason" felt that the reason for 19 psycho terrorists hijacking planes was to unite our country. Fine. But I doubt they thought the unity would last for such a short time. The whole thing just makes me sad. Will there be retaliation? If something else happens to our planes, then Homeland Security sucks ass and all undercover people should be fired. Seriously.

President Bush said tonight this war may take longer than expected. I can't even begin to imagine Dad or Matt being away from home and fighting in a war. Vomit.

Dear Heavenly Father,

Be with the soldiers, those in command, the Iraqi civilians, our nation's leaders, and the families. Give the leaders knowledge, the soldiers courage, the civilians faith in our country's decisions, and the families comfort. Even though this is a difficult day, we thank you for it. I lift up the people in the club. Emily, Christie, Josh, James, Belinda, Dr. Bauer, Grady, Brian E., Ally, her mom, and Mom. Please keep Matt safe on his travels. Thank you. I love you. Amen.

March 25:

I'm heading down to Austin on Thursday—the 24th birthday. It's really not a big deal. Every day, lately, has been a damn good day.

One Problem—My dang cord is leaking. What the hell! Thinking we might have to go to Dallas to get that fixed.

March 30:

Dad's 57ᵗʰ Birthday. He and Mom went to the country this weekend while I hung out in Austin. Wednesday, I got my PICC line re-done. I really didn't think they were going to take it out and do the procedure all over again, but they sure did. No pain. This one works…it's all good.

Thursday was my 24ᵗʰ birthday. 24 seems old. Don't get me wrong—I'm not bitching about birthdays, but right now I don't feel 24. Most of the time, I feel 18. I'm dependent on my parents for rides, I'm at home, and I dress like an 18-year-old. It's just so weird. After college, you are supposed to get out into the Real World, get a job, and live like a responsible adult. I was ready to do that. I was to leave Austin, do something new, and start a new chapter. I know it will be wonderful when I get there, but this has taken a while. This is what I want:

—I want to get in shape.

—I want muscle.

—I want to look good and pretty.

—I want people to look at me because they are impressed with my physical appearance—not because they are shocked by it.

It's the end of March. At times, I feel like I should have optimized this time more. I should have read more or learned friggin' Spanish or Sign Language…but Dammit, I just didn't feel like it. Anywho…

I would definitely say I'm in a weird spot. I feel good about who I am and what I've accomplished, but I don't feel attractive (which right now, I really don't care). I want to have a shapely figure and hair...TODAY...not going to happen.

Moving on—I got some birthday calls from my buds. Martha called. Said she was skiing in Colorado for 2 weeks. No idea how the hell she could afford that when she was struggling for stamps a few weeks ago. Sounds good to me—whatever works.

April 2:

*Oh, it is so fun to feel good and be around people. Really don't have deep thoughts. I've been feeling good, walking more, eating more (should probably ease up on that). I just love it. BOTH LONGHORN BASKETBALL TEAMS ARE IN THE FINAL FOUR. I'm jealous but so pumped for them. I think the guys will win the whole thing and the girls can **so** beat UCONN.*

April 6:

Damn. The girls just lost to UCONN, 71-69. We were up by 9 during the second half. UCONN plays Tennessee in the final. Whoop-de-friggin-do.

The Texas men lost Saturday night to Syracuse. Syracuse plays Kansas in the final. I want Kansas to win, but I think Syracuse is better. Weekend was good. The family and Megan went down to the country.

April 7:

Syracuse won. Good game.

Feeling good, but my ankles are still swelling and my skin is so dry. Dandruff everywhere. Tomorrow I'm going to talk to Matt's girlfriend Megan's softball team about the power of positive thinking.

I did some exercises today. Stretches, leg lifts, dumbbells. It's going to take me a while to get the body back. Longer than I realize I'm sure. Oh, well…it is what it is.

I'm getting some vacations lined up.

San Diego—end of May - June 2 with Sarah

Dubuque—Jill's wedding on July 17th and seeing Meggan's family

New York—after the weddings

Cali—Dave Matthews Concert—July 29th

I really enjoy thinking about this stuff.

Exercise has always been a part of my life. I started playing soccer at age five, tackle football with my brother in the backyard shortly after, competitive basketball in the ninth grade, and I continued to exercise throughout treatment. Being an athlete my whole life, however, almost killed me. I had the walk-it-off attitude during those I CAN'T BREATHE months. I almost walked it off too many times. Being an athlete, however, saved my life, too. My cardiovascular condition kept the tumor from killing me those four months I was being treated for allergies.

Exercise has always given me energy. During treatment, I continued to exercise. Even though my exercise regimen was completely different from what I had been used to as a college athlete, it still provided me with energy. I remember the first time I got up to walk after being diagnosed. First of all, my once athletic legs had shrunk to the size of my forearms. I couldn't believe it. They were so tiny. My dad and I walked out of my room and down the hall about 20 yards. On the way, we passed Bryce, a young man about my age whose leukemia had come back for the third time over six years. The end of the hall seemed like it was miles away. For the first time in my life, I didn't think I could do it. I reached the wall and got back to the room completely exhausted. How was that possible? A year ago I was suiting up for The University of Texas, playing basketball, and in the top percent of physically fit people. Now I was struggling to walk down the hall.

Things got better with practice. The first time I checked into Arlington Memorial Hospital where I would do seven treatments, I measured the hallway at two hundred yards. My goal was to get up and walk a mile every day down the hallway. Some days I could get it done without any problems. On days that weren't as good, it would take me longer. On bad days, I probably didn't finish that mile. But everyday I got up to walk—no matter what. In the ward, I was known as the young one, the basketball player, and that girl who walked the halls.

Exercise was the one thing I could do during the hospital stays which didn't take concentration. That's another thing about the chemotherapy. It makes you so tired you don't even want to concentrate. I did not have to concentrate to walk the halls. Walking gave me a sense of accomplishment. If I walked a mile, I achieved something that day. I walked farther in the hospital than some people do on the outside. That made me feel good about myself. I was proud of myself. Getting up out of bed, gave me a ONE UP on the cancer. If I stayed in bed, I felt as if cancer were winning—as if cancer were getting the best of me. When I walked, I was ahead. I was doing something about my situation.

Exercise gave me a goal. Exercise gave me a sense of pride. Exercise fueled my determination and is one of the reasons why I am here.

Chapter 27 April 15 – August 5, 2003

April 15:

    I don't mean to start out so brash, but this day can kiss my ass. I'll do a lead up to this morning. The weekend was fun. Went to Sarah's Friday night, Gram and Gramps' house on Saturday, and attended this Partylite Candle thing for Megan. I had been feeling pretty good, but tired. I had gotten some Lasix to drain some fluid out of my legs. I peed plenty, but it made me a little tired. Monday, I go to the clinic and they tested my thyroid levels because if that is low it can cause fatigue, muscle soreness, fluid retention, rash—all the things I have. I'll find out tomorrow. Last night, very tired. I went to bed around 9. Woke up in the morning and my face was swollen, skin was red and blotchy, chest looked the same way, and my skin was hot. What in the hell is this? I looked (and still do) like shit. So, I get over looking like I have a severe sunburn and I decided to walk on the treadmill. After about 5 minutes, the nerve damage starts going at it in my back. Whatever it is, it's damn annoying. It doesn't hurt— it's in between hurt and sting. This happens every damn time I exercise. Then, throw in this horrendous rash—not good times. Frustration level has peaked and I'm pissed. What can I do? Cry like a damn baby. I'm so sick of this shit. I have yet to see the light at the end of the tunnel. This really is not a big deal compared to not having platelets, being hospitalized, or having permanent damage like some. But SHIT! Does this ever end? I'm almost 6 months out. I really thought I'd be on my way by now. Not so much. It's crap what people go through to get well.

    Other Frustration—People have no idea. I'm glad they don't. But I'm still dealing with this every day. I get *frustrated when friends or family think I should be ready to go. That's what I would like more than anything—**Ready to go**. Oh my, it's 3 in the afternoon. Again, I've done absolutely nothing, but I feel a helluva lot better than I did 2 hours ago. I was looking pathetic. I still look like shit, but at least my eyes aren't feeling so sad.*

On to other things in the world—The POWs from Texas came home yesterday. I haven't read their stories. I don't know if I want to.

I'm done venting for now. I go to the clinic tomorrow for a test to see if I have blood clots in my legs. Yesssss! What an exciting life. Looking forward to better days…

April 25:

Oh my, Mary Ann is getting married tomorrow.

This past week has been good. I walked 2 miles a few days ago. I was pretty proud of myself. Doctor appointments went well. No blood clots.

Mom and I went shopping this past week. We had a really good time finding things that looked decent on this fabulous body. My health and all of the little things are going pretty good. My ankles still swell, I still have the needle prick sensation in my back, and my skin is friggin' dry. Yep—could definitely do without all of those—Oh, well.

My new goals or ideas:

—Learn now to cook

—Sign Language

—Finish The Power of One

—Yoga

—Check out Pilates

—Check out Masters Programs Maybe I'll check these out before I'm 25.

April 29:

I am cord-free. Yee-Haw. I got the arm thing out yesterday. I'll be able to take a normal shower tonight. No Aqua Guard. No newspaper bags. No ace bandage wrap things. Just me, water, and some soap. Oh, the little things.

Mary Ann's wedding was so fun. She looked great. It was such a personal wedding. No one was shy about hitting the dance floor. It was a really good time.

It's another gorgeous day and I'm going to Gunn Junior High to talk to the 8th grade girl athletes.

May 6:

Today marks my 6 months birthday of the bone marrow transplant. I had my biopsy yesterday and WOW did they give me some drugs. It was great. Dr. Berryman said I'm probably cured. Could use the phrase definitely cured, but "probably" will do for now. Yesterday, I was so doped on the stuff they gave me. Kinda fun but really weird. Slight hangover this morning. I felt like I did on some of the mornings after a night on Sixth Street—putting the pieces of the evening back together.

Today, I was pretty tired. I needed a nap around 3. Didn't do much today, but I'm still tired. Christie called and said she has 12 potential matches. That's great. I hope one of those works out for her. Mom and I were talking about how odd it is to say, "I hope she is able to do the transplant." She sounded great but a little scared. I hope to see her when I get to Austin.

What does this mean? I've been obsessed with watching Romance Movies. I could watch one every day. Action movie with a love sub-plot is great. I love the sexual tension between the characters. I think that means I would like to have sexual tension in my life. Or I would like, at least, to look at a boy and have him look at me with some interest. Whatever. Getting sleepy.

May 10:

Yesterday, Mom and I went to the Relay for Life at UTA. It was so neat. Emily and her mom said a few words. Emily came straight from the hospital. That kid could be one of the toughest I've ever met.

May 13:

And the saga continues. Seriously, does this cancer journey ever end? Yesterday, I went to see Dr. Berryman and he so kindly informed me that the bone marrow biopsy was not perfect.

—PET Scan - Fine

—200 out of 200 male chromosomes—which is good. (Since my donor was a man, I now have XY chromosomes.)

*—BUT the flocytometry (no idea about that spelling) read 0.1% abnormal t-cells. SHIT! Damn 0.1. What the hell is that? Dr. Berryman isn't scared about it, but he is concerned. We'll do another biopsy in one month. At least, I'll get high again. Everything else looks good—all of my counts are fine. I did, however, wake up Monday with another rash. I was just telling Mom and Dad how I think I'm turning a corner (that was Sunday) —maybe not. I **do** feel good.*

I had a great time at Randa's bachelorette party. We went dancing at Have a Nice Day Café which is one of my favorite places. Great music and so much fun. I actually got hit on this weekend by a few boys—older gentlemen to be completely honest—but at least they noticed me. I did look cute. It was fun.

Tomorrow, I'm going to Austin. Tracy graduates.

Oh, walked 2.5 miles today.

Katie and Meg at Randa's bachelorette party

May 18:

One year ago today I graduated from Texas. Damn—that seems like years ago. We went downtown Friday night. That was the first time I have been out in Austin in about a year. Loved every minute. I felt great this weekend. I'm coming back and I'm loving every stinking moment. This is all for now. Doctor visit tomorrow…Shocker.

May 21:

This week is going good. Doctor's appointment went well Monday. I'll go back in two weeks instead of one. Yesterday was a good work out day. Walked 3¼ miles, did some weights, and push-ups. I'm surprised I can actually do a push-up. Ruben won American Idol.

Quick update on the world—We're on High Alert. I still don't know what we are supposed to do with that. Apparently President Bush said some tough guy stuff that is pissing people off. Would you please shut the hell up?

May 24:

Today, I walked a mile in 15 minutes and 2 miles under 32 minutes. I'm getting better. Tomorrow, I'm talking to the youth group at church.

May 28:

Things have been great. I went to Georgetown on Monday to talk to Katie's basketball camp. I'm pretty good at that stuff. Tomorrow, I'll leave for San Diego. I'm so excited. I'll meet Ally. So pumped. She's such a cool girl and has been a source of strength for me. Sarah and I head out tomorrow and return on Monday.

Not so good news—Dr. Deur's wife was in a severe car accident. She is on life support and they don't know if she'll make it. Apparently, this woman is an angel. It's not fair. It's not right. You have people who are getting hurt who are good people.

June 2:

I got back from San Diego today. It was so much fun. Sarah and I got in Thursday around noon. Ally picked us up. Cool, cool girl. I knew she would be before I met her, but she was fun, hilarious and just a good person. We met her parents that night for dinner. Good people. Saturday was the Team In Training Pasta Party. 5,000 people. They recognized alumni, first time marathoners, and survivors. I was so proud to stand up. They had great speakers, great fundraisers, and neat awards. The energy was contagious and I loved it. Sunday was the marathon. Sarah was only going to do the half, but she got motivated at the dinner. Her knee was really bothering her and she knew she couldn't run the whole thing. So, what did she do? She ran 9 miles and walked 17. I was so proud of her. She is such a cutie and such a trooper.

Watching the marathoners finish was so motivating. People who had no business running marathons finished it with smiles on their faces. I cried just about every time someone went by me. It was just so cool to be there with Ally and with Sarah running for me. I know I'll run a marathon one day and it will be soon. How great would it be if Ally and I ran one together? I've got to start making more strides physically—not sure how, but that would be nice.

After Sarah's San Diego Marathon for TNT

My health held up beautifully this weekend. We were out and about quite a bit and I didn't need naps. Victory. I was able to keep up and I didn't hit many low points. I look forward to the day when I can go out there and really let loose...meaning...I'm strong enough to go for a run or proud enough of my body to show it off.

Two things which aren't good—Dr. Deur's wife passed away a few days ago. Her obituary was in the paper today. What an exceptional human being! You read her obituary and you feel so inadequate because of what you haven't done. I want mine to be full of "giving" descriptions like hers. The last line said she will be missed by many, but by no one more than her husband Charles. I can't imagine how much love he had for her when as a patient you feel he loves you with all his heart. Her death is not fair. Again, I don't understand.

The second piece of news is Josh—he is not doing well—not at all. His platelets are down to 5,000. I think he had his spleen removed today. The doctors don't really know what is wrong. He's getting bags of Neupegen and his white count is still struggling. He asked his mom if he was going to die. An 18-year-old kid shouldn't have to ask that. I remember thinking about having to have the transplant and saying, "I don't want to die." Why does this stuff happen? Why is Josh suffering? Is he going to die? I hate even thinking about that question, but, unfortunately, you deal with that reality. Why is Josh having problems and I seem to be doing OK? Why does Emily continue to have to get tumors removed from her lungs. **VOMIT**. I get confused thinking about it.

What's next? I think I'm at a point in my recovery where I can start to do more things and really **LIVE EACH DAY**. More exercise, more projects, more "plans", and crap like that.

This week is a little crazy. Tomorrow night is the visitation for Dr. Deur's wife. Wednesday is another bone marrow biopsy. I think this is #8. Since the last one wasn't perfect, it better be good to go this time. Thursday—recovery day from the drugs. Friday—festivities for Randa's wedding begin.

Dear Heavenly Father,
Please embrace the Deur family and Josh's family. Amen.

June 8:

Great weekend. Randa got married and she looked gorgeous. The wedding was beautiful and classy. I got to see Katie, Frank, Tracy, and Eryn. I went over to Mitra's after the wedding and we went to a med school party. It was such a conquering feeling to be able to go to the wedding after a full day on Friday and still go to Mitra's that night. Finally, I'm getting better every day.

June 10:

Today, Zac was put back in the hospital. They found a tumor by his spine. It's in a different spot from before. They are going to remove it and do radiation. That is what his wife told Mary Ann. Shit! Shit! Shit! What the hell? It's been 3 years since his transplant. I thought he was OK after 3 years.

Dear Heavenly Father,

Please be there for Zac and Dr. Deur. Amen.

June 17:

Tracy's Birthday. She turned 23. I went to Albuquerque on Sunday and came back today. Brian M. and I went gambling. I lost $350. Oops. He lost a heckuva lot more than that. I wasn't bad at blackjack, either. Extremely poor luck. Physically, I'm feeling fine. A little tired, but not bad.

June 18:

Made more travel plans today. I am going to Dubuque, Iowa on July 11th for Jill G.'s wedding. I'll be there for an entire week.

I just read a note from Kathleen on the inside cover of the journal she gave me: "Meg, just a little note to let you know I'm thinking of you. I'm proud of your continuous strength and great attitude. Keep it up and I love you!" My friends are so sweet. So many good people are in my life and I am quite proud of that.

Today was a good day. Walked 3 miles, did my push-ups, and went for a little swim. Pretty tired.

June 22:

I got back from Austin today. I looked pretty cute. I looked healthy. It's so nice to be back doing multiple things during the day and not hurting the next day. My alcohol tolerance is quite good these days. I think it's from the chemo. Thursday I leave for Connecticut. I love it when I tell people I am doing all this traveling and they say, "Must be nice" or "I'm jealous." Dude, I will trade places with you. It "must be nice" looking back and remembering all the chemo treatments. I am just taking advantage of this time of recovery and loving living.

Oh, my former English professor wants to do an article on me for Horns Illustrated, a magazine about UT sports. I'm pretty pumped about that. Maybe this will open the door for other writing opportunities.

June 25:

I feel a little weird about leaving tomorrow. I think since I'll be gone for such an extended period of time I'm not used to it. I'm used to being at home, losing hair, going to the doctor, and not traveling.

The doctor went well today. Normal counts. In 2 weeks, I'll have a long day and a bone marrow biopsy.

July 2:

I am leaving New York and heading back to Connecticut. Oh my goodness, I had the most wonderful time. I arrived in Grand Central Station on Saturday around 11. I met Aunt

Beth at the station. Holy Geeze, there were a lot of people who knew exactly where they were going. I was not one of them.

$165 later we saw The Producers *and* Moving Out. *Incredible.*

After the show, I went to Chelsea to see Sara, a friend I met on my New York trip in December 2001. Apparently, Chelsea is the gay district. Well, that day was Gay Pride Day. I have never seen so many men clumped together with no shirts and big muscles. Quite amusing. Sara has a short hairstyle as well. We definitely looked like we were lesbians celebrating. Had a great time and loved every gay minute. Didn't take any naps and stayed awake until 1 a.m. Getting stronger.

The best part of the day on Tuesday was when Beth and I went to 113th street. We met Sister Mary Christabel and the Episcopal nuns the Starns family asked to pray for me. They were so stinking sweet. How do they do that? They pray all day. Never cuss. Never Drink. No sex. No bad thoughts. No thanks. We met Mary Alice, a nun from Texas. So kind and so happy to be doing what she was doing. She showed us the convent and was grinning from ear to ear the entire time. We got some pictures. So cute. So fun. Spiritual. Uplifting. Healing. Wonderful. Loving.

Meg welcomed to the convent in New York by Sister Mary Christabel

Funny Story—*On the subway ride to Grand Central, I'm sitting there, and who gets on the train? Friggin' Mary Alice. Out of 8 million people in the city, I run into that nun on the same day. The thoughts going through my head—OH GEEZE...IS THIS IS A SIGN? AM I SUPPOSED TO BE A NUN? I'VE GOT THE NAME (Mary Margaret) AND I'VE GOT THE VIRGINITY PART DOWN (Dang it.) ALL I WOULD HAVE TO DO IS STOP DRINKING, EASE UP ON THE CUSSING, AND PRAY A LITTLE MORE. I asked Mary Alice if it was a sign and she said "No." No offense to Mary Alice, but Praise the Lord.*

Right now, I am heading to Connecticut to see Erin.

July 8:

I'm on the plane heading to Dallas. The Cape was gorgeous. Erin's family is great. They were so happy to see me. We hung out for 2 full days. We talked, ate and ate some more. Getting weighed tomorrow at the doctor. Good timing. Leave for Dubuque on Friday.

July 11:

Hello again from a plane. I am in Chicago waiting to go to Dubuque for Jill's wedding. I had a doctor's appointment on Wednesday. Good counts. Got biopsy #9 and got some good Demerol. It doesn't knock me out as long as the Dilaudid, but I still get pretty high.

Thursday, I ran some errands. Mom and I took pictures up to the hospital in Arlington. 10 framed pictures drawn by the kids at the elementary school behind the hospital. They were so cute. The nurses were so excited. One of the nurses said it wouldn't have gotten done if it wasn't for me. That made me feel good. I have to admit after about 50 days of staring at the gray walls of the rooms on the oncology floor of

*Arlington Memorial Hospital, I was determined to liven up
the place.*

July 17:

*I'm here in Dubuque having a fabulous time. I got a little
tired today. I needed to take a 2½ hour nap. Felt better.
Saturday night was the bachelorette party. Oh, that was fun.
Danced all night. Drank too much and had some good times.
Holly (UT volleyball player) and I have been hanging out,
doing nothing, and loving every minute. I got my hair done,
a gift from Meggan's mom. YES…there is enough hair to be
done. I haven't said that in over a year. Got some highlights.
It looks cute. Again, gained some more weight on this trip,
but I really don't care about that. I'm pretty sure I am getting
this vacationing out of my system. I'm not in a routine which
really doesn't bother me, but I'm starting to think about
going back to school, meeting new people, or getting a job.
OK, it's one in the morning. Tomorrow is a resting day before
the big night. Jill is getting married tomorrow. Another one
bites the dust.*

*Got the call that the last bone marrow biopsy was all
clear. My new immune system beat down the 0.1%
abnormal t-cells. Thank you, donor!*

July 27:

*What a great time in San Francisco. Lara and I had a
blast. The first thing we did was go to Chinatown and I got
TWO purses. Yeah, trying to be more girly in my new life.
Not that good at it, yet. We walked a few miles that day. I did
pretty good. Thursday we went to Haight Street. Totally
hippie. People doing pot on the streets. Dirty. Cool Shopping.
I got a cute hat and a sweater from Goodwill. Not so girly.
Oops. We also went to Fisherman's Wharf, saw Alcatraz*

215

(didn't do the tour), and we got some dang good chocolate at Ghirardelli's.

Another great vacation with good people. Now I'm heading to Newport Beach to see Kim and Blake.

By the way, I am so excited to soon have a job, be out on my own, meet new people, and start new chapters.

August 5:

Heading home. Whoa! I'm ready to be back. I had a great time. Hung out with Kim, Scott, Blake, Tracy, and Brian M. (they flew out there, too). It was a full, active trip. We went to Hollywood, ate at Pink's Hotdogs, a place where famous people go to eat fatty hotdogs, and we went to the beach.

I didn't get in the water. I decided that would not have been a good idea. I covered up and put on bottles of sun screen. No burns for me. Pretty sure I was the only person out there sporting the long sleeve look. Oh well. Went to the Dave Matthews concert in Chula Vista. Great venue. Perfect weather. Thank you, Lord, for good days, friends, energy, my donor and safe vacations.

KATHLEEN was a swimmer at UT. She lived two floors down from me in the dorm. She is so cute and so sweet. She reminds me of Katie Couric. Kathleen came to visit me that first week I moved back to Arlington. Kathleen's mom made me "fancy" bandanas which I wore to several weddings. They always fancied up my head. Kathleen always called and her sweetness made me feel so loved. Kathleen would do anything for me.

Chapter 28   August 7 – November 11, 2003

August 7:

Whoa, Nellie. Little fatigued the past few days. I have not put on a bra since I stepped off the plane. Quick update — Belinda died Tuesday morning. She was a few years younger than Mom. Lung Cancer. She didn't smoke a day in her life. Bullshit. The funeral is tomorrow.

August 18:

It's been a while, huh? I can't really say much has happened. I was utterly wiped out from my trips and I think I picked up a little cold. I have a cough, scratchy throat, and I'm completely exhausted. The weird thing is when I breathe, I hear this raspy, wheezing sound. The sound reminds me of 2 years ago when I heard that exact same sound for the first time. This time, I went to the doctor and had a chest x-ray. Everything was clear. But this wheezing thing when I take a deep breath should be clearing up soon. I'm going to give it a couple more days for it to go away. If it's not gone by then, I might start to get worried. My counts are fine. It's just weird and we all know what happened the last time things were weird.

August 25:

For the first time in a long time, I had a great, energizing day. I went up to visit Scarlett at the clinic. She is such a sweet girl. She is going to have an auto transplant soon and she wanted to talk to someone who had gone through a transplant. It is such an unknown thing and you want to know what to expect.

September 7:

I haven't been feeling the greatest here lately. I have had this raspy thing going on in my chest. I went into depressed/scared mode the other day. My breathing is not getting better. My chest was sounding like it did in November 2001. I started to think about the tumor coming back and how much that would register beyond shitty. All this got me thinking — I could have done without this cancer thing.

I had a good cry with Dad. It was good he was there with me. He got to hear what I was thinking directly and not through Mom. It was a moment.☺

On Monday, I started exercising. I have walked every day this week except Saturday. I have started to feel better and I think walking is part of it.

Friday was Arlington High's Homecoming. Miss Emily was crowned the queen. She stood out there at midfield with her short hair, her one arm and her smile. A few tears were shed. AHS is such a good school, with a great principal, and great kids. They didn't vote for Emily because she has cancer. They voted for her because she is a good person and has inspired us more than anyone could imagine.

September 13:

The week was pretty good. I kicked myself in the ass on Tuesday. I had a good workout and pretty much overdid things. I was worthless from 4 on Tuesday until Thursday morning. The exercise is going well as long as I don't try to get a six-pack, quad muscles, and triceps in one day. Stupid. It seems like each time I feel like I should be out getting jobs, the next day I'm exhausted and needing a nap at noon. It seems like I try to figure out every day where I am physically. I don't know why I do that. I know I'm not THERE yet, but I constantly test myself. I feel like I should be doing something. I should have a job. I should be out of the house. I should be meeting friends. Then, I realize I'm just not up for it right now. Don't get me wrong…I feel good and I'm not bitching about that…it's just the same thought of What the hell is going to happen?…and …What am I doing? Those are always fun questions I have no idea how to answer. So, I need a project and I'm really hoping Dr. Deur will want me to organize an effort to decorate the infusion room at his clinic. It's gray, dull and drab—just what cancer patients need to lift their spirits.

September 28:

Wow! 2 weeks without an entry. That must mean I'm doing things besides writing in my journal. I love it. I started tutoring Caroline, Mary Ann's youngest sister, in algebra.

I wrote a letter to Dr. Deur letting him know the infusion room needs to be painted. If I haven't heard back from him in three weeks, I'm thinking it's a No.

Emily Hunter was honored as Texas Person of the Year by American Cancer Society. That's not the right title, but it's something like that. It's well deserved.

I talked to the Bowie High School girls basketball team last week. It was really fun. I enjoy doing that stuff.

I'm starting to think about life/career options. Do I want to teach? What kind of kids? What grade level? Do I want to go back to school?

Basically, here is what I am interested in:
—P.E. Teacher
—Going to grad school for Masters and teacher certification
—Leukemia and Lymphoma Society
—Masters in Leadership
—Motivational Speaker

—Helping Cancer Patients
—Helping At Risk Kids
—Going to New Zealand for teaching

October 12:

Recovering from Texas/OU weekend. We got spanked. 65-14. Yikes. Friday, is the start of the Planet Cancer Retreat for young adults. I'm feeling great. I have determined my energy level is back to 90%. I went the entire weekend without a nap—kinda. Today, I took one, but that was a recovery nap. OK, I really didn't go the entire weekend—just Saturday—whatever. I'm feeling good...so good it's time for bed.

October 22:

Friday through Sunday was the Planet Cancer Retreat. Awesome. So fun. Worth it. I would do it again. It was cool to be able to talk to people who knew what was going on without having to go into all the details. We did talk about cancer quite a bit, but it wasn't depressing. No one was angry or bitter. It was life. Our lives.

October 26:

First things first—Matt asked Megan to marry him. Third engagement has got to be the charm. They are a good match for each other. Megan is a keeper and everyone welcomes her to the family.

This weekend I went to Camp John Marc, a camp which families of children with cancer were attending. The first girl I saw was about 6, bald, and had the prednisone face. I felt like someone had hit me in the stomach. It made me so sad to think this girl and thousands of other little kids are doing the same things I had to do. I wanted to tell the families, "Hey,

I'm one of you. I know what you are going through." It's weird how you're part of a club you don't want to be in, but at the same time, you want to let others know you're a member—just like them.

November 6:
Happy Unbirthday to Me. I had my transplant one year ago today. It really is unbelievable. To think that last year I was at Baylor, bald, probably getting ready to puke, and had just received my donor's cells. I went back and read my journal entries from last year. It seems so vaguely familiar. Thinking…was that really me? Did I really go through that? There was so much uncertainty with every day. Was I going to feel like complete crap? Was I going to puke? Would I get Graft vs. Host? Would this be my cure? Looking back, I honestly did not know if I would get here—November 6, 2003—healthy, living a "normal" life. Sometimes thinking about the past confuses me. It's like I know it happened because I saw it in a movie—not because it happened to me.

Mom and I had a great weekend in Austin doing the Race for the Cure. Mom and I had a moment. We truly know how lucky we are.

Praying for Emily and her family. Mom and I saw her yesterday and she was jaundiced. She was still talking, smiling, and laughing, but hardly had the strength to do so.

Dear Lord,
Please be with her sister, brother, mom, and dad. They need you now more than ever. Be with her friends in the days and weeks ahead. Thank you.

November 10:
Emily update—She is at home and hanging on. They are having a graduation ceremony for her on Wednesday night.

She is to the point now where it might be a matter of days.

Josh update—Not so good. He's having trouble getting off the ventilator and his platelets have dropped again. I don't really know what to think about this and I sure don't know what to say.

November 11:

Emily, with her empty sleeve, in a locker at Arlington High

Emily Hunter passed away this morning in her sleep. She was at peace and had no pain. I really don't know how I'm feeling about the whole thing. It was weird to see her picture on the news and her not give an interview. This morning, I could only think of her transition period. She was here and then this morning she was on her way to eternal life. It's simply not fair. She fought so hard. She was young. She had the positive attitude. She was strong. She did everything she was supposed to do and it still didn't turn out the way it was supposed to turn out.

Dear Heavenly Father,

Even on sad days, we thank you for them. Be there for Emily's family. I know she is looking down on us with hair, two arms, strong legs, and that heart-warming smile. Give her a hug for me and give her our love. Amen.

PLANET CANCER is a young adult support group for cancer patients. It was founded by **HEIDI ADAMS**. Heidi was 26 years old when she was diagnosed with Ewing's sarcoma. Like many young adults, and like me, she was misdiagnosed for several months. After treatment and a return to health, she decided to make a difference in the young adult cancer community.

Because young adults are the "forgotten" group in the cancer world, Heidi has offered an outlet for those patients. On the web site www.planetcancer.org, Heidi provides message boards for fellow patients to discuss their treatments, their frustrations, and to share their anxieties about the future. Every year, she has a retreat for young adults to get together, to talk, to bond, and to have fun. Heidi wanted to make a difference in the cancer world and she has.

I have never considered myself a lucky person. I have never won even a dollar in the lottery. My name has only been drawn once out of a raffle. At the sixth grade carnival, I won a gift certificate to the pet store.

Now getting cancer shortly after my mom had cancer— I wouldn't really call that lucky.

My family and friends, trying to lighten the moment, would joke about how lucky I was. They would say things like, "Meg, you are so lucky, you don't even have to shave your legs," and "Meg, you are so lucky, you have such a cute, round, bump-free head."

After knowing several people with my disease and my mom's disease pass away, my family realizes how lucky we are to be alive. As unlucky as we both were to get cancer, we are a hundred times as lucky to have survived it.

Since being diagnosed, I have met and become friends with fifteen people who have died from cancer. These people had all the same advantages I had. Emily, for example, had the best doctors, the positive attitude, and the faith. She had more people loving her than we could ever imagine. People prayed for Emily in the same breath they prayed for me. Emily continued to play soccer despite her imbalance. Emily just didn't have the luck.

When I tell people my story, the most common response is "You are so blessed." Yes, I am, but are the people who died—were they not blessed? Yes, I am blessed, but I am also very, very lucky.

Chapter 30

November 15:

Today was Emily's funeral. I would say a thousand people came. It didn't seem like a funeral. It felt more like a celebration. I know that is what funerals are supposed to be like, but this was different. I felt like we were celebrating a victory. Emily's victory. That's pretty cool that a 17-year-old can have that kind of an impact on a community.

As I was thinking about Emily, she reminded me of why I'm not exactly ready to go into the classroom. I think I can impact people the way Emily did. I want to "make a dent" in the world—like Emily would say—and I don't want to be ordinary. I'm not saying teaching is ordinary, but it can be. Doing what I want to do…working with sick kids, at risk kids, special needs kids isn't ordinary. I want to inspire, encourage, and impact people, but I don't want to do it in the classroom just yet. OK, I'm off my box. Good night and hugs to Emily.

November 25:

One year ago today, I came home from the hospital. Wow!!! I remember coming home and only eating Melba toast. Not the best of times. Thanksgiving is in two days. I am so thankful for family, friends, Dr. Berryman, nurses, medicine, technology, my donor, love, laughter, the healing body, healing spirit, good people, loving people. I'm thankful for every breath I take.

December 1:

Thanksgiving was wonderful. Thirteen people came over. That's a lot for our little family. I'm feeling good. I have four substituting jobs this week. That's 300 bucks. Yahooooo. I am slowly making money. The only thing to kinda complain about is my knees and ankles. They don't really feel too good most of the time. I think it's about time to start some physical therapy.

December 13:

This past week I have been a math tutor at junior high and I really enjoyed it. I am figuring out I love being with kids and hearing what they have to say. In big groups, I would prefer them in a P.E. setting. I like the junior high and high school kids because they are at a more impressionable age.

December 31:

Vomit. I just found out Scarlett passed away this morning. She was 28.

January 1, 2004:

So, it's a new year. Peace out 2003. No more cancer. No more big-time recovery. No more holding back because of cancer. I'm going to live like a "normal" 25-year-old. It's going to be a good year for our family. Thank you, Lord, for this day.

Tomorrow is Scarlett's memorial service. She got real sick over last weekend and by Monday they called hospice. Her liver failed and nobody knows why. Her cancer was still active, but I don't think they expected this. Scarlett was a cool girl. So sweet. All the nurses just loved her. I feel a bit removed from it—if removed is the right word. I have noticed

I have felt this way more and more with deaths due to cancer. I don't have this overwhelming feeling of sadness…it's a more accepting feeling and just knowing death is a possibility.

Andrea, Meg, Mary Ann at Andrea's Party

January 2, 2004:

Oh my goodness—it's 2004. That's crazy. Four years ago, we were bringing in the New Year at my apartment with the basketball team and everyone was scared the world was going to blow-up because of Y2K. Two years ago, I was in New York with Lara having the time of my life. Last year, I celebrated with Morgen, bald, and high on steroids. Oh my… I went out to Fort Worth to celebrate Andrea's birthday. We had a few Saki Bombs. I think I might be allergic to alcohol. I have broken out in a rash the last few days and the only thing different has been alcohol consumption. I really hope that is not the case.

Let me back track a few days. For New Year's, I went out

229

with Mitra. We had a really good time. Went to a house party and then headed downtown. I would say I wasn't drunk-drunk, but feeling pretty darn good. In my tipsy state, I told one of Mitra's friends that I would like to do a half-marathon for The Leukemia and Lymphoma Society in her friend's honor. So, it looks like I'll be doing a half-marathon. I can't take it back now. Mitra's friend got a little emotional about the whole thing. Good one, Meg.

January 18:

My former English professor who is writing the article about me for Horns Illustrated *came up to talk to Dr. Berryman. Dr. B. told Professor Buckley about the chances for a transplant to work.*

One-third of the transplants don't work and the patients die; one-third work, but the patients die of infection or complications from Graft vs. Host Disease; one-third work and the patients survive. YIKES!!!! I'm glad I didn't know that beforehand. Matt told me the other day the oncologist in Austin told him my chances were about 30%. I never really thought about percentages. I always thought I was going to be fine. Dying didn't even enter the picture. Geeze, it feels like I have been doing this cancer thing my entire life. Walked 6 miles today. Will be feeling it tomorrow.

January 21:

I am subbing or babysitting today at a junior high. As a sub at the junior high or high school level, your job is not to teach. You make sure no one gets killed and that includes the teacher.

I applied to The Hole in Wall Gang Camp—camp for kids with cancer.

January 26:

This weekend I became certified to become a ropes course facilitator. What was I thinking? I don't think I totally thought the idea through. Jenny at Camp John Marc told me about it because most of the qualifications for jobs I want mention ropes course training. I think I originally thought we would meet on a ropes course and learn how to climb. I think one would understand why I would think learning would be part of it since I was the one who needed to learn everything. I was completely wrong.

Here we go:

There were 9 of us. 8 of us had experience. One did not. Most of us were Recreation & Leisure Majors. One of us was not. 8 of us knew how to climb, tie knots, belay, and rescue. One of us had absolutely no idea. It was like me going to a computer seminar with computer geniuses. I was a bit out of place.

So, Friday night as we are stretching, I'm wondering if I am going to be able to do this. Again, I had reason for concern since I pulled my hamstring trying to stretch my quad. Yikes!

Saturday we started climbing. I have never climbed anything and now after a year of chemo, I'm trying to do this. Again, what was I thinking?

With my first step on the telephone pole staple, my foot cramps. Great. I haven't even done anything yet. I continue to climb and reach the top. I seemed to be more focused on my legs giving out and my feet cramping than making sure I am locked up and not falling to serious injury. Later that day, we had to climb to the top of a pole, climb over and on top of what seemed like a 4' x 2' platform, and stand up. I have trouble getting up off the floor with help. It was a sight to see, but I did it.

It was a fun weekend. Don't think I'll be going to the reunion, but it was fun. It was definitely a learning experience. I was challenged. My body was challenged. I passed and I am quite proud of myself.

I have joined Team in Training. I will do a half-marathon in Dallas on May 16. I am going to do it in honor of Josh and in memory of Mitra's friend. She died fifty days after her transplant.

February 1:

I had a great weekend. Saturday, I went to physical therapy. I have decided I am going to do this three times a week. Getting involved in a program like this should help the stiffness.

Oh, Ms. Panton's art class from AHS is going to paint Dr. Deur's infusion room on March 27.

February 6:

What a busy week! Tutored, subbed, went out to dinner, and worked out 3 days this week at 6 a.m. Whew! It's great to be alive.

Interviewed with the people from Hole in the Wall Gang. I think it went pretty well. Looking forward to working there this summer.

March 15:

Sitting at Baylor, waiting for Dr. Berryman. Nothing is wrong. I'm here because I want to know if something can be done about my lack of flexibility. I know—minor problem, but it's not getting better. I've been going to physical therapy for two months and nothing has improved. The other night Dr. Mitra felt my arms and thinks there is a fascial build-up or something. My tissue is lumpy. If this is part of IT, that's cool, but I just want to see if something can be done about it. If that means stretching more or massage therapy or physical therapy—whatever—I'll do it. My stamina is great. I just can't put on my own socks. That's a slight problem. So, Dr. Berryman wanted to see me before I made any decisions. Good call.

Done with the doctor visit. Here is the deal:

I might have some Graft vs. Host stuff in my muscles. Dr. Berryman called it chronic. Not a big of fan of that word or group of words. What that means or what I think it means is the graft from my donor is fighting my cells in the muscles. That explains why they are inflamed all of the time. I am going to try an anti-inflammatory drug and try out massage therapy for a while. Dr. Berryman is such a wonderful man.

March 20:

Friday, I had an MRI on my legs. On Monday, I will have a deep tissue massage. They need to rub some of that crap out of there. I saw a few physical therapists today and they said I have severe muscle tightness. Yeah—got that.

This morning I met up with Team in Training and had such a good time. What a great group of people. We walked 9 miles. It was excellent.

March 31:

I had a great birthday. 25! Thank you, Lord, for another birthday. Saturday, I went to the team walk—10 miles. Then, I headed to the clinic to meet Ms. Panton and her art class. It looks so good. The kids did great. There were about 30 or 40 kids who showed up. They painted fourteen murals. I cried every time I looked at a new picture. Kids definitely thought I was a weirdo. Oh, well.

Tuesday, I had a massage. OUCH. Those aren't going to feel too good.

233

Meg applauding the art students

April 8:

Still no word on the camp. DOH!!! If I don't hear by next week, I'm outty. I'll be totally disappointed and shocked really. What in the heck am I going to do? Oh well. No sense worrying about it.

Update—George Bush and his Iraq plan sucks. Over thirty people have died this week and it's getting worse. He has some ultimate plan (pass the rule/control over to Iraq by June 30). Not going to happen. Hard to pass control over when you don't have it in the first place. What hacks me off is he doesn't back off anything he says. He can't admit when things have been miscalculated and he just keeps pushing. That is all. I pray for our troops.

April 13:

Still no word on the camps.

I went to the Cooper Clinic today and got a good report. Dale, the PT, told me that my condition is recoverable. He definitely could feel the tightness problems in the muscles and just as much in the joints. He thinks the water therapy I am doing should be beneficial, but he also thinks I need hands-on therapy—more than the massage. He also wants me to see a Neurologist Physical Therapist something doctor. Yeah—made that up. He basically thinks I can get better. He is really the first one who has said that. Most people have just said, "This is just part of it." Screw that. I realized the other day I can't do most of the activities which used to be so natural. No basketball, softball, volleyball, running, rollerblading, or just moving athletically. I know it'll take time. It's still hard for me to understand my body went through pure hell. I can get back to where I was. Lance Armstrong did it. Other people have gone through this and don't feel handicapped.

April 14:
Okie, Dokie—I've got today and tomorrow to hear from the camps. I don't have a good fallback plan if this doesn't work out. Maybe I can find some experiential education jobs or something and it'll give me a chance to see if I like it. I'll be a little disappointed if I don't hear from them. I won't feel rejected or anything, but they're missing out on a good one. So, what am I going to do with my life—at least next year? I know the month of May is going to be my Rehab/Get in Shape Month.

April 15:
Today is when I am supposed to find out about the camp. I think I found out. No job. I am a little bummed about that.

April 22:
Heard back from the camp. They didn't have me as a camp counselor. Helper in Woodshop. Yeah—no thanks. I told him I already took a job this summer working with kids. Tiny white lie. Oops. Technically, I will be working with kids at the basketball and softball camps, and giving private

lessons—just not in an organized camp-like situation. Oh well. I did figure out that I should eliminate the possibility of an experiential education job. Physically, I can't do ropes climbing, I can't run after kids. I can't do a lot of the stuff that would make that job reasonable. I seriously thought about doing something like Outward Bound. Yeah—that's not going to happen. In order to do that, I would have to be a) in bad-ass shape b) strong enough to lift anything and the body just isn't ready to handle that kind of demand. I just want my body to be back to normal. I want to run. Jump. Stretch. Rollerblade. Swim. Dance. Bend down and pick something up off the floor—without pain. This might be the price of living, but right now, I refuse to accept that. Anywho, so rock climbing, ropes course, backpacking, and anything which could lead to falling might not be the best of ideas right now.

Here is my ideal job: P.E.—how it's supposed to be. Kids learning how to play sports and learning how to be healthy. I have seen P.E. programs run like Wellness Programs and I love it.

April 26:

Epiphany—I want to move back to Austin and teach P.E. Yep!! That's the deal. I just decided this a few days ago. Teaching gives me benefits, a salary, experience. I want to gain some experience so I can teach at schools like the Andre Agassi School in Las Vegas. I just need to get my foot in the door. I need a year of experience. I am pretty excited about the possibilities. I've made some good contacts and I am feeling confident about it. Why go back to Austin? I love it. The P.E. programs are more advanced. I know a few people down there. I love the town. It is a good place to get started.

April 28:

Sent in my resume to Austin and Round Rock. Very excited about this.

Chapter 31   May – December 2004

May 5:

Happy Cinco De Mayo. Mom and Dad are in Hawaii. It's been nice having the place to myself.

*The teaching thing might not be happening for the fall. I don't have my teaching certificate. No certificate = Problems. I really think there is a way to get hired. (Although I had enough hours to get my degree when I left school, I didn't finish my student teaching. So no certification. And I **did** fail the teacher Excet test on Feb. 16, 2002, just as I predicted.)*

May 8:

Horns Illustrated *came out today. It's really good. People really liked the journal entries. Professor Buckley did a great job. He said he was going to send it out to other magazines and to Oprah. How cool would that be?*

May 13:

OK, for real, Lord, we need to have a talk. Mom has been feeling like crap. She and Dad just got back from Hawaii. She was sick the entire time. Dad has had something for three weeks. Mom went to the doctor today. On the way, she had double vision. So, they had to do a friggin' CT scan on her brain. Lord, we are not doing this. Nothing is wrong with her. Please, let this be just a virus or something. We can't do any of the big crap right now. Basically, I am just praying that you watch over her. Give her physical strength. Please.

May 17:

Mom is much better. Not really sure what was wrong, but she is better.

The half-marathon was so much fun. The weather was perfect and the course was nice and flat. The people involved in TNT are so cool. There is so much positive energy and they are truly happy that the participants feel good about themselves. Dad and I walked in at just under 3 hours. That's a little less than 14 minutes a mile. That's pretty damn good.

May 22:

I went down to Hutto for a job interview today. I don't know about teaching in Hutto. It's a cute town. I'm sure it's a good school. It's about 30 minutes, at least, from Austin. My instincts just say, "No Thanks" and I'm trying to think of reasons to validate it. The main reason would be their health insurance might not cover me under Dr. Berryman. I want to stay with him for a few more years. More later…

Today, I was really tired. I needed two naps. I haven't had to do that in quite a while. I guess I was tired from the week. It was pretty busy. About the job situation—it would be really nice if something happened in that department. I have put in my resume, application, and references to Austin, Pflugerville, Round Rock, Hutto, Georgetown, and every other city around Austin. I really want to teach this first year so I can get certified.

Saw the movie, Love Actually. *Love it. So cute. So wish I had someone feel that way about me and me about them. It would be fun. Good night.*

May 25:

Teaching Situation—I got the job in Hutto. That's good, but I don't want to teach in Hutto. And the deficiency plan at UT won't work for teaching in Hutto. In order for the deficiency plan to work, I have to teach P.E. and P.E. only. This job is science. P.E. is such a specific job and the openings are limited. The coordinator of Austin schools thinks something will happen, but it could take all summer. I don't think I have all summer. So, as of today, I wouldn't say I am that confident. Honestly, I have no idea what is going to happen. I know things are going to work out, but REALLY—is it going to happen and when? (Big Sigh.)

MRI report—I do have fascia damage in my forearms. That's good news. I think. No GVHD. I just need to get serious about stretching.

May 27:

Okie, Dokie—Not the best day. I thought I wasn't going to have any more of these. We have moved on to Plan F for my life. Today, I had a reality check. I went to see a specialist about my stiffness. She checked out my MRI and wants to know why I have fasciitis and myositis. As we were talking, I wasn't getting the feeling that this was going to be done with or that I would be able to run, jump, and play in a few months. I asked her if the problem were treatable and how long did she think it would take to see improvement. "With diligent stretching—9 – 12 months." Not bad. I then told her about my desire to be a P.E. teacher and what did she think about that. She said doing that in the fall would be very, very challenging. She said I would have to develop skills that would teach the children without me showing them what to do. Basically, I would have to teach a kid to teach other kids. She's right. I can't show a kid how to jump, how to shoot, run a three-legged race, long jump, serve a volleyball—the list goes on. In the back of my mind, I had my doubts. I wondered if I would be able to do it. Thinking about controlling 50 kids and not being able to bend down to tie their shoes overwhelmed me. It looks like the teaching door is closing for me. I don't want to teach science, math, or English—or whatever. I want to teach P.E. or Health. In order to teach Health, I would have to go back to school and get about 18 hours of it. I am going to sleep. I'll finish tomorrow.

May 28:

I'm back. Things are much better today. It's a new day and the spirits are up. The conclusion from yesterday is this: I won't be teaching in the fall. P.E. just isn't going to happen. I wouldn't be able to withstand being on my feet all day. My feet cramp after just a few hours of being on them. How could I teach all day, 5 days a week? I couldn't. So, I have told the professors at UT I won't be doing the deficiency plan in the fall. I'll be looking for something else. I was pretty sad yesterday. Not because I wasn't going to achieve my lifelong dream of teaching, but because I'm, AGAIN, not able to do something I want to do because of f*^#ing cancer. Excuse me.

I was in the vacation room yesterday and Mom lay next to me crying and said, "Why did this have to happen to you?" It was awful. I felt so deflated. I felt like we were sick again. It was one of those days that was just sad. I thought I wasn't going to be sad anymore. I guess I always thought I would deal with cancer and be done with it. I would return to normal because in my mind, I thought, "This isn't that bad. I'll get through it and everything will be fine." In the big picture, everything is fine. I'm cancer-free and healthy. Even saying, "I'm cancer-free" is just weird. WHAT? I had cancer? Still can't believe it. I guess because I don't understand it.

Anywho, today was a good day. I feel good and

energized. I know I'm being led somewhere. I have been led away from teaching and on to something else. Maybe writing a book. Maybe The Leukemia & Lymphoma Society. Motivational speaking. Who knows? I know it will work out and I'm still excited about the possibility. This is just a little step back. But thank you, Lord, for my health, my family, my friends, my donor, and my life. Amen.

June 5:

I've seen a PT that specializes in myofascial release. I've received 2 treatments. I can't say I feel tons better, but they believe it's going to work.

Mom and I talked the other day and we're both thinking the time still isn't right to move away. It's quite obvious the body has some work to do. Also, I want to write THE BOOK. That would not happen if I moved to Austin in a month.

June 15*:*

The tightness is definitely not getting better. Played golf with Gram today. First hole, make my putt, bend down to get the ball out. I can't. I can't lean over that far to get the ball. My legs won't let me. What the ^&%$? So, I had to ask Gram if she could get the ball for me. It's quite humbling to ask your grandmother to lean over and get you something. I am supposed to be helping her. Played well but a little frustrated. Really hope this gets better soon.

July 14:

I met a guy named David today. He's a sophomore at Texas A&M. He was working at a Christian camp out of state. On his way home to Arlington, he got in a car accident. At the hospital the chest x-rays showed a tumor in his chest. It was non-Hodgkins lymphoma. I've decided to walk San Francisco in his honor.

241

August 1:

It's August and it's bleepin' hot. I'm starting to get a little tired of my hour and a half drive to PT. It blows the entire day. And I don't know if it's helping. I feel no different than I did a few months ago. If anything, it might be getting worse. Dr. Berryman says I have chronic GVH. Great. The GVH has settled in my muscles and joints. We don't know if it will get better with therapy, or time, or if it will ever get better.

I had a moment last week. I am tired of not being "normal." I know I'm not going to be like I was in college. I'm not even asking for that. I don't give a damn about my jump shot. I want to get off the toilet without needing to hold on to the walls. I watched some AAU basketball last week. As I watched, I thought, "Did I really used to play basketball?" It's really frustrating and I really would have been OK without the cancer.

Weird—Yesterday, I walked 12 miles and my feet didn't appreciate it at all. They look like hell right now. No idea what the hell happened. They have this blood blister look to them. No idea if I was cutting off circulation with my socks. Walked too much? GVH? It's all a mystery. When is it not?

Well, it's noon and I am still in bed. Definitely a no bra day. Time for lunch.

August 20:

Mom had her three year anniversary today.

September 15:

I'm sitting in Arlington High's foyer subbing for the yoga teacher. Since I had trouble getting up off the mat, I probably didn't help the kids much today.

Job update—I am going to be the Junior Varsity and

Assistant Varsity basketball coach at The Oakridge School. So, I'll tutor math during the day in public school and then come over to this private school and coach. It's something. It's money. I'm excited.

The body and its tightness—not getting much better. I'm definitely worse at yoga today than I was six months ago. DOH! I'm starting to lose feeling in my legs—to the touch. It feels like I have been given numbing shots. Not good.

October 12:

Kinda had a rough weekend. I was all excited about the Texas/OU game. Friday morning I woke up and my eye was red. Real red. It didn't get much better throughout the day and by Friday night, it was almost swollen shut. I decided not to go out because I had already done that whole I LOOK DIFFERENT FROM EVERYBODY ELSE thing. So, I didn't go out and I missed a really good time with the girls on Friday. Saturday, I tried to catch up with them all day, but I didn't see them until 10 that night. I was getting more and more pissed off by the minute thinking of the reason why I hadn't seen them yet. My eye was jacked from my new medicine to help with the tightness which is from the transplant because of fucking cancer. The medicine also makes my face super dry. Not cute. Fucking cancer. I was tired last week because I started all of my new jobs since I hadn't had a job because of fucking cancer. Needless to say, I have been in better spots in my life.

October 26:

What a trip! Just got back from San Francisco. Walked my second half-marathon. It was awesome, but, oh, those hills. The best part was the Pasta Party. I talked at 12:30 to about 1,500 TNT participants. I nailed it. It was close to perfect. They laughed, cried, and gave me a standing ovation. I'm really good at that stuff and I love doing it. I am hoping something comes from it.

A year ago, I wanted to do a race with Ally. Now I have because Ally walked the course with me.

Ally and Meg after walking the half-marathon
in San Francisco

November 1:

Two years ago today, I was admitted to Baylor — getting ready for the transplant. That seems like 10 years ago. I feel 35, not 25, and it continues to feel like it happened to someone else.

November 3:

I think George won. Pretty amazing so many people still like him. There was a poll done yesterday and 21% of the voters said they vote on morals, and out of those, 70% voted for Bush. I really don't understand that one. Does John Kerry not have morals? Just because he thinks gays should have rights?

November 9:

Coach Greene has leukemia. Shit. I heard he is still working.

November 15:

I'm getting better. I can pick up stuff off the floor. I'm going to be normal. Thank you, Lord.

November 19:

My health seems to be getting better. I was able to wash my feet for the first time in several months. That's some improvement.

November 29:

Good news. In our basketball practices, I am starting to feel capable. Today I shot the basketball. Yes...I actually looked like a basketball player. I had a follow through and everything. A few months ago, my arm couldn't straighten and if I shot the ball, it would hit the underside of the rim. Today, the arm was straight, the form was good, and the ball went over the rim. It was great. Too bad I was only about 2 feet from the basket, but I'll take it.

I'm feeling one day not too far off I'll be able to do "normal" things. How great will that be!!!

Another improvement: I was able to get down on the floor and play with the dog. YEA!!!!

December 10:

Today, I found out about my donor. All I knew before was that my donor was a 31-year-old man. The marrow donor program protects the identity of donors and recipients for one or two years, depending on the country. Now I know his name is Marco. He lives in Germany not far from Berlin. Thank you, Marco, for saving my life.

Meg with Matt and his wife, Megan, "that internet girl"

Chapter 32   January – December 2005

January 2, 2005:

Omigosh! What a New Year celebration! Lara and I went to LA for the Rose Bowl. First of all, I can't believe it's 2005—Sheesh. Second of all, Texas won the Rose Bowl, 38-37. Dusty Mangum kicked a 37-yard field goal with 2 seconds left. Vince ran for 191 yards and 4 touchdowns. He is a god. Unbelievable game. So fun. Great seats. Think I peed my pants. Loved it. Hook 'em!

February 19:

Today, I took the Math Excet test. I decided to listen to Dad. He's right. If I pass the test, I'll be more marketable. If you can teach math, you'll always have a job. The P.E. and health window seems to be getting smaller and smaller. The test wasn't that bad. It was to certify me to teach 4th through th grades. It was harder than I thought it was going to be, but not bad. Hopefully I passed and this will help me get a job, get money, and get my own place.

March 15:

I passed the math test! Ya-hoo! Now I'm certified in math, P.E, and health. For the love, I better get a job.

March 28:

Friday, Mitra calls and says she has skin cancer. Shit. That's just great. What in the hell? The invasion is level 4 which is usually a stage II. Not good—but not awful. She still has bleeping cancer. Damn. What are the chances that two friends would have cancer before they turn 30? Seriously, I was supposed to take care of everyone. No one else I know is supposed to get cancer.

May 17:

*GOT A JOB. EULESS JUNIOR HIGH. 8TH GRADE
MATH AND 9TH GRADE BASKETBALL. $44,000/YEAR.
YEE-HAW!*

*GOT AN APARTMENT. SO NICE. 10 MINUTES
FROM SCHOOL. MOVE IN JULY 5. VERY EXCITED.*

June 16:

*David died today from non-Hodgkin's lymphoma. He
was 20.*

Meg with David

DAVID died a month before his 21st birthday. David
and I had the same disease. His tumor was in the
mediastinum, the same spot as mine. We experienced
similar symptoms. We had the same chemotherapy
treatment.

I only knew David for a few months. Every time I saw
him, he was smiling, laughing, talking about his wonderful

friends. David reminded me of me. His family reminded me of my family.

David went into remission for several months. During this time, he returned to college at Texas A&M, returned to his friends, and returned to his life. His remission only lasted a few months.

After his relapse, the only treatment option left for David was an unrelated donor transplant. The chemotherapy drugs he took after falling out of remission were stronger than the drugs the first time around. His recovery was longer and took a toll on his body. David developed an infection and went into ICU before the transplant could take place.

Days after a donor had been found through the National Marrow Donor Program, he passed away.

David shouldn't have died. From the moment I met him, I knew he was going to make it. He had wonderful doctors. His smile exuded a positive spirit. When people talked about David, the first thing they mentioned was his faith. People loved David. Over a thousand people came to his funeral. David was more active during his treatment than I was. A lucky David would still be here.

If I ever get upset because I can't touch my toes or because of the cost of all my pills, I think about David. I think about how David and his family would love it if his muscles were tight and he had to take ten pills a day. I think about how lucky I am to be here.

David made the most of his time here on earth, and I feel certain he is doing the same in his life after cancer.

July 1:

Talked to Joy the other day. (I heard about Joy when someone with Team in Training ran in her honor. He asked me to visit her. Joy had her transplant in September 2004.) She sounded great. I have never heard her sound that good. She is such a sweet person.

Going to Dubuque tomorrow to be a bridesmaid in Meggan's and Justin's wedding. So friggin' excited. It's going to be incredibly fun.

July 9:

I moved into my new apartment yesterday. Ya-Hoooooo!!! It is so nice. Huge. Tons of space. It's so nice to be moving on. About time. It's nice to feel like a grown-up. It is a bit weird not seeing Mom and Dad every 20 minutes, but I'll get used to it.

Meggan's wedding—The ceremony was perfect. Meggan looked beautiful. Everyone was so happy. The reception was an Absolute Blast. So fun. Danced for 5 hours. Great people. Fun people. Inspired me to think of opportunities to throw a party. Love it.

July 16:

The apartment is awesome. I am loving it. It is so fun to be at home doing whatever I want, watching TV, talking on the phone at midnight, walking around naked. It's great.

August 21:

The second week of school starts tomorrow. It's great. It's fun. I'm tired. More later.

September 12:

Been a little busy. Loving school. Loving coaching. Life is good. Going to Maui on Friday to walk in the half-marathon and give the speech. Haven't walked in 2 weeks and haven't practiced the speech. Oops!

September 19:

It's 10:10 p.m. in Texas and we are on our way back from Maui. It was a blast. Burnt the hell out of my shoulder. &*&^%. What's a little melanoma?

I finished the half-marathon right at 3 hours. We started at 5:30 a.m. It was a beautiful walk by the ocean. I walked by myself most of the time and I really enjoyed it. I spoke at the pasta party on Saturday night. I did good—really good. Standing ovation. Love that. So, I'm going to school in 8 hours. Now, I'm trying to figure out what the heck I'm going to do for the lesson. I'm loving teaching and the kids are great. My principal said he could tell I was born to teach.

December 10:

Coach Greene's funeral was today. He passed away Tuesday from complications of the unrelated donor transplant which put him in remission from leukemia. He had a transplant a few months ago and it didn't work. It f-ing sucks. I get mad and sad all over again. Coach Greene was such a good guy. Every time a friend dies, it reminds me how lucky I am to be here. That could have been me and who knows why it wasn't.

In other news, Joy is not doing well, either. She has been in the hospital for a month, and she has been unconscious for most of it. They don't know what is wrong with her or what happened. They don't know if it's from the medicine or if it's GVH. The doctors told the family three times she won't make it through the night, but she has. I don't know how many more times she can do it. She was doing so well. I thought she was in the clear. I don't know if I'll hear anything. Again, this pisses me off. If she passes, this will be the third friend in six months. I hate this.

COACH GREENE was the boys junior varsity basketball coach at Arlington High School for many years. He was energetic, funny, fun-loving, carefree and competitive—all the things which made high school kids love him.

He loved the University of Texas and the Longhorns. He went to Austin every chance he got. We always connected with each other because we both could talk about basketball, and he loved it when I signed with Texas.

Coach Greene grew up in Arlington and attended Arlington High School. He played on the basketball team, and his dream was to be the head coach at his alma mater. He accomplished his goal a few years before he was diagnosed.

If the world were perfect, Coach Greene would still be here. He was a fighter. He was positive. He had faith and people loved him. The thousand people who came to his funeral included fellow teachers, church members, current and former students and players, and friends. He was a good guy. Coach Greene just wasn't lucky.

If I ever get upset because I can't shoot the ball like I used to, I think about Coach Greene's family and how they would love to hear him complaining about his jump shot.

Coach Greene always made people laugh, and I know he is continuing to do that in his life after cancer.

December 26:

We had a wonderful, loving Christmas. I was really emotional yesterday. Cried at church. Baby-cried watching It's a Wonderful Life. Mom and I listened to Kenny G…I bawled. I was just so grateful and happy. I started to think about David's family and Coach Greene's family and how sad they are right now. Then, I thought about how sad my family would be. I really am grateful. Things could have easily been very, very different.

This journal has lasted me about a year and half. I used to go through a journal in a few months. It's nice to be busy. I really love not having the time or the need to write in this every day. Life is good. Thank you, God.

December 28

I found out today that Joy died.

Dear Heavenly Father,

Thank you for my life. Thank you for everyone and everything in my life. Thank you for being my friend and always being there for me.

Lord, I am hoping you will do me a favor. Will you please let Doug B., Baby Ally, John D., Dayton, Amanda, Bryce, Mitra's friend Nicole, Mrs. Breault, Coach Greene, Belinda, James, Scarlett, Joy, David, and Emily know they are always in my heart, and I think of them often. As I pray, I cry. I cry because my life is so good. I cry because I am happy, and I cry because I wanted them to be happy with me.

Lord, one more favor. I know I'm pushing it. I am hoping you will always shine your light down on my friends who are still in The Tough Club with me: Grady, Ally, Ally's mom, Brian E., Christie, Heidi, Audra, Josh, John B., Meaghan, Zac, and Mom. Please give us, and all survivors, the strength to face cancer not just with courage and determination, but with joy and laughter. Help us to keep dancing with the enemy as we refuse to let the bad times outweigh the good. Amen.

Afterword   May 6, 2006

This day marks three and a half years that Marco's immune system has resided in my body. Even though I am experiencing some complications, I love Marco and his immune system. Because Marco's system has latched itself to my skin (graft vs. host disease), my skin feels about two sizes too small. One physical therapist told me, "It feels like you are wrapped in saran wrap." This prevents my muscles and joints from having total freedom of movement. The upside is my new immune system is tough enough to fight off the mutating t-cells which caused all my trouble in the first place. I have only had that one unclear bone marrow biopsy six months after the transplant, and Marco's immunity took care of that.

The only other side effect of treatment I'm dealing with now is the development of cataracts. I'm right on schedule for this as a by-product of Total Body Irradiation. I didn't really think I would beat the grandparents to cataract surgery, but I've got to always remember I don't have cancer any more.

Today I am healthy. I have a ponytail. I am now able to run, to play basketball, and to retrieve a golf ball from the cup without my grandmother's help. Although I don't do these activities very well or half as smoothly as I used to, at least, I am capable. Admittedly, no one would call me limber, but the condition is slowly getting better.

Because I am back on medicine (the dreaded prednisone) which suppresses my immune system, I visit the doctor every three or four months. I continue to take eight to ten pills a day. I still wash my hands just as much now as I did during treatment. Although Dr. Berryman told me patients do fall

255

out of remission after three years, the likelihood of that happening to me after so long is slim—very slim. YES!

I currently work in a germ-infested environment and have yet to miss a day because of illness. I teach eighth grade math and coach basketball. I love it. Teaching is natural for me. Being around people is natural for me. I guess I did make the right choice, after all.

My mom is still in remission four years out of treatment; my dad is thrilled I have a job with benefits; Matt did, indeed, marry Megan in 2004, and they are expecting my first niece or nephew later this year.

You might have guessed, but I am single, have no kids, am an Aries, and if you are a man with no criminal record, I'm probably interested.

I am also a motivational speaker. I enjoy it because I am good at it. I am passionate about my story and passionate about sharing it. I love meeting the people who hear it. My goal today and every day is to be grateful. Gratitude brings appreciation, happiness, positive attitude, faith, and love. I love my life—all of my life. I love even the cancer life because of the people I met and the opportunities which will evolve.

I don't know where I'll be in twenty years, or five years, or even next year. What I do know is TODAY I'm alive, and I am CANCER FREE TODAY AND EVERY DAY FOR THE REST OF MY LIFE.

In Memoriam

The following people "fought the good fight" as the cliché goes. These fathers, mothers, brothers, sisters, grandparents, husbands, wives, and friends had everything I had. They learned from the best doctors. Their glass was half-full. People loved them.

They knew the importance of exercise. Prayers were lifted up for them by many of the same people who were praying for me. They simply did not have the luck.

One of the good things about cancer coming into my life was I was fortunate to meet so many wonderful people who shared my experience. The ultimate bad thing was that cancer never left some of the bodies of those who I laughed with, talked with, walked with, and shared with.

My friends who I feel certain are making a difference in their cancer-free life above:

Faye Brown (my grandmother)
Doug Doggett
Belinda Lozier
Allan Jacobi
Alice Breault
Perry's wife
Dayton
Chris's wife
Doug B.

Bryce
Coach Greene
James
David
Scarlet
Joy
Emily
Christie
Zac

About the Author

Meg Brown was born in Arlington, Texas, moved to Austin for college at The University of Texas, taught two years in Euless, Texas. In 2007, Meg returned to Austin where she teaches math and physical education at the Ann Richards School for Young Women Leaders. In May 2008, Meg competed in the Capital of Texas Triathlon—her first—with Team in Training. See her website at http://www.megbrown.org/ to invite her to speak to your group.

Meg and her mother

July 2002, Virginia   July 2002, Brian E.

July 2002, Erin & Tracy

October 2002, Dad   July 2003, Jill G. & Holly

July 2002, Aunt Beth

November 2003, Race for the Cure
Christmas 2003, Mom

The Leukemia and Lymphoma Society

Portions of the proceeds from sale of this book go to support Team in Training of The Leukemia & Lymphoma Society. To contribute directly to research in blood-related cancers (leukemia, Hodgkins lymphoma, non-Hodgkins lymphoma, multiple myeloma), go to lls.org or send donations to

> The Leukemia & Lymphoma Society
> P.O. Box 9031
> Pittsfield, MA 01202-9031

Bone Marrow Donation

Of all the patients needing a bone marrow or peripheral stem cell transplant, over 70% of them do not have matches within their families. Meg was one of the lucky 70% because two of the 5.5 million potential donors across the world had bone marrow close enough to Meg's to be called perfect matches. Many patients do not have matches, particularly those patients of non-European descent.

To add your name to the database of person's willing to save a life by going through a relatively mild process, go to marrow.org or contact your local blood center. Marrow donation drives can be held along with blood drives within your communities. Donors must be 18- to 60-years-old.

QUICK ORDER FORM

Telephone Orders: 866-465-7073

E-mail: sales@getumotivated.com

Online Orders: www.getumotivated.com

Postal Orders: Motivated Proformance Inc.
628 Canyon Rim Dr.
Dripping Springs, TX 78620

Name: _____

Address:_____

City:_____ St_____ Zip_____

Telephone:_____

Email:_____

Sales Tax: Please add 8.25% for orders shipped within Texas addresses.

Shipping: $3.85 for first book and $2.00 for each additional.

To schedule a speaking engagement contact Susie Gold, 866-465-7073.

Author Contact: www.megbrown.org